The Everyday I Ching

The Everyday
I Ching

SARAH DENING

St. Martin's Griffin ⚮ New York

Library of Congress Cataloging-in-Publication Data

Dening, Sarah.
    The everyday I ching / Sarah Dening.
        p.   cm.
    ISBN 0-312-15122-5
    1. I ching.   2. Philosophy, Chinese.   I. Title.
PL2464.Z7D45   1997
299'.51282—dc21   96-47906
                                                CIP

First published in Great Britain by Simon & Schuster, Ltd.

First St. Martin's Griffin Edition: March 1997

10 9 8 7 6 5 4 3 2

Acknowledgements

More people than I could possibly mention here have helped to make this work possible. I am grateful to all of them. In particular, I would like to acknowledge Richard for uncomplainingly cooking the meals whilst I became a workaholic, Ian Fenton who inspired me to write this book in the first place, Shirley Dixon, Georgina Eden and Mary-Ann Pereira for their love and unfailing moral support, and last but by no means least, Ean Begg for his constant encouragement on the Way.

Dedicated with great affection and gratitude
to the memory of C. G. Jung

The Everyday I Ching

Introduction

The *I Ching* or 'Book of Changes' originates in China and dates back to at least 3000 BC Like most very ancient wisdom it was for a long time transmitted orally. It is reputed to have first been written down around 1123 BC by King Wen and his son, the Duke of Chou. Later on, the great sage Confucius added his own commentaries.

What is the *I Ching*? It is a guide to the best way of dealing with any particular situation in life. The Chinese invented the compass as a way of orientating oneself in the physical world.* Likewise, they created the *I Ching* to help us to point ourselves in the right direction in daily life. Based on the principle that everything changes constantly, it teaches us how and when and where to act. A highly practical book, the wisdom it contains is as compelling as that of the Bible.

Until about a hundred years ago, the *I Ching* was more or less unknown in the West. Recent years have seen it grow in popularity, together with other aspects of classical Chinese culture: Taoism, Buddhism, martial arts, acupuncture and herbal medicine. Chinese systems of healing, in particular, are the focus of ever-increasing interest in the Western world. Why is this? Unlike Western medicine which sets out to deal with the symptom, the Chinese approach is concerned with the underlying cause. This, in their view, can only be correctly diagnosed by examining the entire energy field of the patient. Such a holistic view of the body is appealing to a growing number of people. In our highly mechanized and 'hi-tech' society, perhaps we prefer to be treated as something more than machines whose components, when they go wrong, must be repaired or replaced.

To understand how the *I Ching* works, we may compare it to the practice of

* My thanks for this metaphor go to Dr Anne Maguire.

1

acupuncture which is based on similar principles. The acupuncturist focuses on the flow of energy in the body. Where there are imbalances or blockages in the flow, illness will eventually result. When appropriate corrections are made in the energy field, the body is restored to the optimum conditions for healing itself. The *I Ching* deals in similar fashion not with the body but with the situations we meet in life. These too are regarded as fields of energy in which various forces are at work, creating a particular state of affairs. So if we want to change the situation, we must first do whatever is needed in order to change the underlying energy flow. This will benefit the situation overall, just as the acupuncturist's needles affect the whole body. The *I Ching* identifies the forces at work in the situation and recommends the most appropriate action or attitude under the circumstances. In other words, it tells you what needs to happen in order for things to change for the better.

How does it do this? In Chinese thought, there are two basic principles in life, the masculine or *yang* force and the feminine or *yin*. (If you are interested in computer language, you will recognize this as a binary system). The *I Ching* contains 64 hexagrams, or figures of six lines in different combinations. There are two types of line, broken and unbroken, representing the yin and yang principles. The hexagrams, each of which has a name, are said to depict every possible type of situation one may meet in life. This means that any situation you meet will be made up of a particular combination of yin and yang forces. A successful outcome, as we have seen, is the result of identifying the forces and correcting any imbalances.

The great psychologist C. G. Jung, in his brilliant foreword to the classic translation of the *I Ching* by Richard Wilhelm, claimed that it works according to what he called the principle of synchronicity, or meaningful coincidence. In other words, when you throw the coins, the way they fall has meaning. The resulting hexagram reflects the wisdom which already exists in your unconscious mind but is largely hidden from view. By concentrating on the situation and using the coins, you can gain access to these deeper levels. And it is probably true to say that using the *I Ching* over time will have the effect of increasing your powers of intuition.

Just why is the *I Ching* particularly relevant to us today, in the West? Each of us experiences change, day in and day out. Life is the same in this respect today as it was for the individual who lived a thousand years ago. In the Chinese culture, change was always regarded as an intrinsic part of the

2

flow of life. As Westerners, we can learn a great deal from this approach. In our search for security, we may try to hang on to a job which doesn't fulfil us, a relationship which has served its time – or our youth as we grow older. We tend to experience change as threatening rather than challenging. As a result we often fail to see the possibilities inherent in a new situation. The *I Ching* indicates how we can cope with change in the most intelligent and harmonious way. With its help, we can become experts in the art of being versatile. In today's rapidly changing world, this ability is needed probably more than ever it was in times past.

The *I Ching* is NOT a book of fortune-telling. Nor is it a substitute for your own common sense. It is meant for giving guidance in situations where you are uncertain about the best direction to take. Use it well and it will enhance your life as though it were a wise and trusted friend.

How to Consult the I Ching

What you will need

In addition to this book you will need pen, paper and three coins. If you can find them, use Chinese coins which are round with a square hole in the centre. These can sometimes be obtained from bookshops (two of which are detailed at the back of this book). But any three coins will do, provided they are of the same size and value. Before using the coins for the first time, you may like to wash them thoroughly, or soak them in salt water. This serves to purify and dedicate them for use with the *I Ching*. Keep them specially for this purpose, preferably in a box or wrapped up. Do not let other people handle them.

Making your preparations

Relax and allow your mind to become quiet. Then focus on the question you want to ask. Many people like to create a ritual to help them get into the right frame of mind. This can be something very simple like lighting a candle, settling into a comfortable position and taking a few slow, deep breaths.

Asking your question

If you want an understandable reply, you must ask a clear question. Avoid the either/or type of question. For example, 'Would it be to my advantage to take the job with Smith and Co.?' is a precise question. 'Should I take the job with Smith and Co. or wait until I hear from Jones Ltd?' would be too muddled. Alternatively, you can ask the *I Ching* to give you its views on a situation – 'Would you please comment on the difficulties I am having with Jane', for example. The answer will indicate the most constructive way to deal with the matter.

Making the hexagram

Shake the coins in your cupped hand and let them fall on to a flat, uncluttered surface. Traditionally, heads has the value of three and tails counts as two. If you have Chinese coins, the side inscribed with figures counts as two and the reverse side as three.

You will receive one of four possible combinations, each of which is then represented by a broken or unbroken line, as follows:

Three tails	$3 \times 2 = 6$	—x—
Three heads	$3 \times 3 = 9$	—o—
2 tails + 1 head	$2 + 2 + 3 = 7$	———
2 heads + 1 tail	$3 + 3 + 2 = 8$	—— ——

Write down whichever of these lines you have received. It now becomes the *bottom* or *beginning* line of your hexagram. Keeping your question in mind, repeat this process five more times. Add the lines one on top of the other until you have built up a hexagram or figure of six lines.

Example

Place of line in hexagram	Combination of coins thrown	Total value of coins	Type of line
Top	3 heads	9	—o—
Fifth	2 heads + 1 tail	8	—— ——
Fourth	2 heads + 1 tail	8	—— ——
Third	2 heads + 1 tail	8	—— ——
Second	3 heads	9	—o—
Beginning	2 heads + 1 tail	8	—— ——

6

Identifying your hexagram

Now you are ready to find out which hexagram you have drawn. The lower three lines are called the 'lower trigram'. The top three lines form the 'upper trigram'. In the example above,

the upper trigram is   ——O——   and the lower trigram is   —— ——

                  —— ——   ——O——

                  —— ——   —— ——

Ignoring the markings 'O' and 'X' (think of these lines for now simply as broken (—— ——) or unbroken (————), turn to the Chart at the back of the book. Look at the row of trigrams going across the top (each described by a Chinese name) and find the one that corresponds with the upper trigram in our hexagram. Now look in the vertical row of trigrams down the left-hand side of the chart and identify the one which looks like the lower trigram. The box where they intersect contains the number of the hexagram we have made. You will find that it is number 4 which is called INEXPERIENCE. Interestingly enough, before writing this section, I asked the *I Ching* for a demonstration hexagram to help people to learn how it works. It came up with – INEXPERIENCE!

The moving lines

You will notice that the second and top lines in our practice hexagram are marked with a circle. This indicates that they are 'moving lines', so called because they change into their opposites. The solid ———— changes into a broken —— ——. When a hexagram contains moving lines, the next step is to change these into the opposite type and construct a new hexagram. Here is what happens in the case of our example above:

      ——O——   →   —— ——

      —— ——   —— ——

      —— ——   —— ——

      —— ——   —— ——

      ——O——   →   ————

      —— ——   ————

Follow the instructions above to identify the new hexagram. You will find that it is number 2 which is called RESPONSIVENESS. I would take this to indicate that the more responsive you are to this new system, the more successfully you will learn. If you look at the section 'Making the hexagram' (p. 6) you will see that there is another type of moving line, the one which has the value of 6 —X—. When this appears in a hexagram, you must change it into its opposite, ——— and construct a new hexagram as above.

Only lines with the value of 6 or 9 – three tails or three heads – are moving lines and therefore subject to change. Lines with the value of 7 or 8 stay as they are in both hexagrams. The second hexagram will contain no moving lines.

If all the lines in your hexagram have the value of 7 or 8 then there are no moving lines. In this case, you will have just the one hexagram to study. It means that no immediate changes are on the cards. For the moment, the situation is fairly static.

Reading the hexagrams

1. The first hexagram comments on the current situation which is discussed in the first two sections of the text. If you have received only one hexagram, do not read any further.
2. If you have received moving lines, move to the third section, 'Further aspects of the situation' and read the text for your particular moving lines. It gives additional information about changes which may be in the air. In our example the relevant further aspects would be 'Nine in the second place' and 'Nine at the top'.
3. Then look up the second hexagram. This tells you about future possibilities once the changes have taken place. Again read the first two sections of the text but this time do NOT consult the third section. Remember, this deals with moving lines only.

Do not be disheartened because this process sounds complicated. Just follow the instructions step by step, be patient and practise. Once you have consulted the *I Ching* a few times, you will understand just how easy it is to make a hexagram. In no time at all you will be rewarded for your patience in learning this procedure. The *I Ching* will rapidly become an invaluable source of advice which will help your life to flow in the best possible way.

8

Some do's and don'ts

* DO approach the I Ching with respect, as you might a wise friend.
* DO ask your question with an open mind. If the answer you get is not the one you wanted to hear, remember that the I Ching is concerned with helping you to do the right thing. It has no interest in propping up your ego!
* DO consider keeping a special notebook for recording your questions and answers. This will help you to develop your friendship with the I Ching over time.

* DON'T ask your question when you feel distracted by other things. The I Ching tends to respond to whatever is most on your mind at the time. Unless you have cleared your mind of distractions, it may well comment on those rather than on the question itself.
* DON'T use the I Ching as a party game. Its purpose is to give you guidance when you have choices to make. If you just ask it silly questions, it will give you nonsensical answers.
* DON'T keep asking the same question over and over again. If you do, you will be quite likely to receive hexagram number 4 (INEXPERIENCE) which is the I Ching's way of rapping you over the knuckles! The only exception to this is where you are involved in a situation which is static. In this case, you may want to ask from time to time if there are any changes in the air.

1

The Creative Force

'I must Create a System, or be enslaved by another Man's;
I will not Reason and Compare; my business is to Create.'
William Blake

Success is assured when you draw this hexagram. Provided that your goals are worthwhile and not merely selfish, significant achievement is possible. Make this a time of great activity. Use your initiative to set your plans in motion. Others will look to you to take the lead. A high level of confidence will give you abundant energy. Use this for the benefit of all concerned. You can find creative ways to resolve problems and accomplish ambitious goals. Look ahead. Be aware of the consequences of your actions. Good timing is essential. Do not allow yourself to be pressured into taking action prematurely. Consolidate your position of strength by refusing to waste your resources on trivial or irrelevant issues. Be positive and determined to achieve your aims. Do not get involved in anything unworthy of you. This is a most favourable time. Be sure to make the most of it.

An opportunity for personal growth

Dynamic energy, unless it is used wisely, can be destructive. The more power you have, the more careful you must be not to abuse it. In the current situation, you are in a position of considerable influence. Direct this to positive ends and you will be a source of inspiration to others. Use it negatively and you could create havoc. Take responsibility for your actions. Be supportive of others. Beware of over-ambition and excessive pride. Be especially sensitive to other people's feelings. Take their views seriously. Be kind and tolerant. If matters do not go exactly according to plan, be patient. Guard against arrogance and look for opportunities to learn.

Further aspects of the situation

NINE AT THE BEGINNING
Be patient. The time is not yet ripe for action. As yet you do not fully understand what is involved. Wait until matters become clear. Until then, keep a low profile.

NINE IN THE SECOND PLACE
Aim high. Your abilities qualify you to make a major contribution to the situation. But you are not yet in a position where your value can be fully appreciated. It would be to your great advantage to cooperate with somebody who is already involved in your field of interest.

NINE IN THE THIRD PLACE
New opportunities are offered. With your goals firmly in mind, make careful choices based on what feels right for you. Do not be concerned about pleasing others or trying to satisfy their needs. Know your priorities and refuse to be side-tracked. Do not be over-ambitious.

NINE IN THE FOURTH PLACE
You are at a crossroads. You can take a higher profile in the situation or withdraw from it so as to pursue other interests. Neither path is in itself better than the other. Your choice depends on what best suits your

12

temperament. If you are true to yourself and follow your intuition, you will make the right decision.

NINE IN THE FIFTH PLACE
This is one of the most favourable positions of all. It indicates that you can accomplish almost anything. Make full use of all your resources. Aim high and do the very best you can. You have considerable influence. Use it well.

NINE AT THE TOP
You have become too ambitious. If you push matters any further you will lose touch with reality. You have to know when to hold back. This will protect you from the danger of going to extremes. Remember that pride comes before a fall.

Note: When all the lines have the value of nine, every aspect of the situation is changing. The Creative and Receptive Forces are perfectly balanced. Exceptional good fortune is indicated. Your influence will be extremely beneficial.

2

Responsiveness

```
━━   ━━
━━   ━━
━━   ━━
━━   ━━
```

'O Lady! we receive but what we give,
And in our life alone does Nature live.'
Coleridge

A responsive attitude is the key to dealing with matters at this time. Do not try to take control of the situation or to initiate action without consulting others. The result would be confusion. But this does not mean that there is nothing you can do. On the contrary, you must make choices and take decisions. What matters is how you go about it. Have an open mind. Be prepared to listen and learn. Try to discover what the situation most needs. Find out what would best serve the interests of those involved. Armed with this information, you can decide what kind of contribution you can usefully make. Be generous and willing to serve others. You have abilities and resources which could be of great benefit to all concerned. Discuss the issues involved with friends and others who can help you to carry out your decision. Very great success is indicated.

An opportunity for personal growth

The most valuable resource you can draw on at this time is your intuition. This still, small voice within is all too easy to ignore. Yet it represents an inner source of wisdom which can guide you in the direction you need to go. This is a natural, instinctive type of knowledge and has nothing to do with working things out in your mind. But the pace and the noise of everyday life can make it very difficult to hear. Try to make some space in your life to be alone and reflect on the situation. It will give you an opportunity to tune in to what it is that you really want, need, think and feel. The views of other people are invaluable. But unless you have a clear idea of where you yourself stand, you will simply become confused.

Further aspects of the situation

SIX AT THE BEGINNING
Keep a close eye on developments. Be patient. Accept that matters must be allowed to proceed at their own pace. Be on the look-out for the very first signs of things going wrong. If you can nip problems in the bud at the beginning, you will save yourself trouble later on.

SIX IN THE SECOND PLACE
You do not have to put on a show or go out of your way to make a special effort. Being who you are is enough. Just do what needs to be done in a simple, straightforward way. If you are true to yourself and act naturally, you will instinctively do the right thing.

SIX IN THE THIRD PLACE
Do what you have to do quietly and efficiently. Don't seek credit for your efforts at this stage. Your abilities will be recognized and rewarded in due course. Meanwhile, just concentrate on doing your best.

SIX IN THE FOURTH PLACE
Trouble is brewing. Be extremely cautious. Keep a very low profile. Avoid doing or saying anything which might lead to confrontation. Keep your ideas, thoughts and feelings to yourself.

SIX IN THE FIFTH PLACE

Be tactful and discreet. Do not draw attention to yourself or try to impress others with your achievements. A low-key approach will bring you great success.

SIX AT THE TOP

Do not get involved in a power struggle. If you insist on being competitive, you will create serious difficulties for yourself and others. Be flexible and willing to cooperate.

Note: When all the lines have the value of six, it indicates that success will be the result of your ability to stay with things and see them through. Your willingness to persevere in the face of difficulties will give you great inner strength.

3

Difficulty in the Beginning

```
═══   ═══ ═══
═══   ═══ ═══
═══   ═══ ═══
═══════════
```

'In the middle of difficulty lies opportunity'
Albert Einstein

A new cycle is beginning. This means that you cannot avoid change in some area of your life. Things which until now have seemed important may no longer have the same meaning for you. You find yourself questioning beliefs which you have previously taken for granted. The situation is confusing. You are venturing from the comfort of what is familiar and safe into unknown territory. There are so many different possibilities that it's hard to know what to do for the best. You would benefit from the advice of someone who has the experience to understand your predicament. In the end, you will have to decide for yourself what to do. But at present you are working in the dark and could do with help in casting some light on the situation. A more experienced point of view will help you to clarify your own thoughts and feelings.

An opportunity for personal growth

The challenge is to deal with impatience. You may be tempted to jump at the first opportunity which appears to offer a way forward. Such a move would be premature and bring trouble. Stay calm and wait. In the ancient text, your position is compared to that of a blade of grass having to push up through the earth to the light of day. It can only do this when it has grown strong enough. But the process of growth cannot be hurried. In the meantime, hold back and conserve your energy. It is only a matter of time before your course of action becomes clear. Rest assured that, in the end, there will be a highly successful outcome.

Further aspects of the situation

NINE AT THE BEGINNING
Right at the start you have encountered an obstacle to your plans. Although you are determined to succeed, you must not try to push ahead regardless. To deal with the situation effectively, you need to take advice. Be open-minded. If you are prepared to listen and learn, you will find the help you need.

SIX IN THE SECOND PLACE
The situation is frustrating. You would like to forge ahead but cannot. Out of the blue, an unexpected solution is offered. You may be tempted to grasp it as a quick way out of your difficulties. But the offer, although perfectly genuine, is not the right one for you at this point. You could eventually end up paying a high price for acting hastily now. When the time is right, the help you need will come from the right quarter. Until then, be patient and wait.

SIX IN THE THIRD PLACE
Because you are on unfamiliar ground, you do not have the experience to deal with the situation. Under these circumstances, any action you take will only make matters worse. For now, give up chasing after this particular goal.

SIX IN THE FOURTH PLACE
The situation is too difficult for you to deal with on your own. You need help and it is available. But it is up to you to make the first move and ask for the assistance you need.

NINE IN THE FIFTH PLACE
You know what must be done to resolve the situation but circumstances are such that you must be very cautious. Stay in the background and take one step at a time, using the utmost tact and sensitivity. In the end, your patience will be rewarded.

SIX AT THE TOP
You have been offered an opportunity to leave behind an unsatisfactory situation and move on to better things. Yet you feel that it is all too much for you. Such a defeatist attitude must be overcome at all costs. Nothing is holding you back except yourself.

4

Inexperience

‘As far as we can discern, the sole purpose of human existence is
to kindle a light in the darkness of mere being.’

C. G. Jung

Because you lack experience of the issues involved, you feel confused. You
don't know what to do for the best. You need to ask for help. But advice
is only useful if you are prepared to listen. This means putting aside any
preconceived ideas of your own. There is no shame in not knowing all the
answers. Keep an open mind. If you genuinely want to learn, you will get
the information you need. INEXPERIENCE can also indicate that there
is no point in asking this question. It may be that you already know the
answer perfectly well and there is nothing more to be said. Alternatively,
as often happens, you have already consulted the *I Ching* on this point.
The answer you received was not the one you wanted. And so you keep on
asking in the hope of being given something more to your liking. This is
no more acceptable to the *I Ching* than it would be to a person you kept
on pestering with the same question.

An opportunity for personal growth

Be prepared to learn something new and perhaps unexpected. Ideas you cherish may now be turned upside-down. If you are unprejudiced, a new area of understanding can open up to you. When asking for help, you do not have to prove to whoever you are consulting how clever you are. You are there to learn. Nobody will be willing to carry on teaching a person who thinks that they know it all anyway. A far more intelligent approach is to assume that you know nothing. Then you cannot help but learn. Depending on the situation, it may be that you are the one who has been approached for help. If you sense that what you have to say is falling on deaf ears, do not feel obliged to continue. It is of no benefit to you to waste your time in this way.

Further aspects of the situation

SIX AT THE BEGINNING
If you seriously want change for the better, be prepared both to learn and to put those lessons into practice. Otherwise you will just skate across the surface of things and achieve nothing substantial. Exercise self-discipline but not to such an extent that it stops you from enjoying life.

NINE IN THE SECOND PLACE
If someone has made a mistake, do not be judgmental. Put yourself in their place and show some compassion. Remember how difficult it can be to do the right thing. Be patient and tolerant.

SIX IN THE THIRD PLACE
Do not be over-ambitious. Keep calm and be patient. Listen and learn. Proceed one step at a time. Do not compromise your self-respect in an effort to get too much too soon.

SIX IN THE FOURTH PLACE
Be realistic. If you are too proud and stubborn to listen, the result will be humiliation.

21

SIX IN THE FIFTH PLACE
Because you are open-minded and genuinely willing to learn, you will succeed in achieving your aim.

NINE AT THE TOP
Someone who constantly refuses to learn may need to be punished for their mistakes. This is the last resort. If you are the one who has to exert discipline, be objective and remain emotionally uninvolved. Go only so far as is necessary.

5

Waiting

——— ——
————————
——— ——
————————
————————
————————

'All things come round to him who will but wait.'
H. R. Longfellow

You must wait patiently, trusting that everything will work out as it is meant
to. Owing to factors beyond your control, no direct action can be taken at
present. But this does not mean that you should simply do nothing. You
must use this time of waiting in the right way. Stand back and get an
objective view of the matter. Look at things exactly as they are and not
as you might like them to be. Wishful thinking is useless. Once you can
see the situation clearly and unemotionally, you will understand why you
have had to wait. At this point, the best way forward will start to emerge.
Then and only then should you take action. During this process, you may
come face to face with your doubts as to whether you can succeed at all.
Do not worry. Keep your goal firmly in mind. When the time is ripe, you
will attain it.

An opportunity for personal growth

Your inner security is being put to the test. To try and force a situation which is not yet ready to happen would be a great mistake. You could lose ground you have gained. You must accept that you just have to mark time. Meanwhile, try to use this period of waiting creatively. Take care of yourself, physically and emotionally. Build up your strength and your energy. Cultivate a good, positive attitude. This will help you to counteract the stress involved in waiting. Focus on living in the here and now. Having to wait does not mean putting your life on hold. On the contrary, it is important to enjoy yourself to the best of your ability. Appreciate all that is good in your life.

Further aspects of the situation

NINE AT THE BEGINNING
Be patient. Take care of business. Even if you feel uneasy, rest assured that problems are a long way off. Do not be anxious.

NINE IN THE SECOND PLACE
If people gossip about you, or try to draw you into arguments, let it pass. Do not get involved or try to defend yourself. This would only make matters worse. Stay calm and quietly confident. Keep in mind what you aim to do. The situation will improve.

NINE IN THE THIRD PLACE
You have caused trouble for yourself by rushing ahead impatiently, without considering the consequences. Now you are in a vulnerable position. It is still possible for you to extricate yourself. But you must keep a cool head and be extremely cautious. Carefully consider the possible effects of any step you take.

SIX IN THE FOURTH PLACE
The situation is critical. You cannot move forward or go back. All you can do is stand fast and allow events to take their course. It is essential that you

stay calm. An emotional reaction will not serve you. To have any chance of getting out of this situation, you must do nothing which might involve you further in it. If you wait patiently, you will be able to extricate yourself in due course.

NINE IN THE FIFTH PLACE
You are offered a temporary respite from difficulties. Take the opportunity to relax and enjoy yourself. Recharge your batteries in preparation for the next step. But do not be self-indulgent. Keep the balance between enjoying the moment and remaining determined to achieve your goal.

SIX AT THE TOP
The time of waiting has come to an end. Now you are beset by difficulties. There appears to be no way out. All your efforts seem to have been in vain. However, there is an unexpected turn of events. Help is offered, although it may come in an unusual or unfamiliar form. You may therefore be wary of accepting it. But the offer is genuine. Take it, and there will be a happy outcome.

6

Conflict

```
━━━━━━    ━━━━━━
━━━━━━    ━━━━━━
━━━━━━    ━━━━━━
━━━━━━    ━━━━━━
━━━━━━    ━━━━━━
━━━━━━    ━━━━━━
```

'No one wins a conflict unless both feel understood and enlightened
about the theme or the nature of the other.'
Arnold Mindell, *The Leader as Martial Artist*

Conflict can arise because you have not made your position clear from the
beginning. This is a lesson to bear in mind for the future. Once you are
involved in a conflict, you are faced with finding a solution. Stay centred
and keep cool. An aggressive approach will only make matters worse. Before
making a move, ask yourself what you are hoping to achieve. Do nothing
which might work against this. Where there is a breakdown of trust, an
impartial point of view is needed. This may mean involving somebody who
can be trusted to act as a mediator. The most successful outcome will be if
everybody involved feels they have won something. For this to happen, you
must be willing to give the opposing point of view a fair hearing. Do not
start new projects or make major changes in your life until the conflict is
resolved.

An opportunity for personal growth

There is nothing to be gained by prolonging conflict to the bitter end – even if you are in the right. It will only serve to increase bad feeling. If neither party is willing to compromise the situation can only deteriorate. Whereas if you are prepared to meet the other half-way, a solution can be found. Your pride may suffer a little, but a flexible attitude under these circumstances is a sign of strength. It does not mean giving in. On the contrary, you must support your own case. But this does not prevent you from listening to the other's point of view, and trying to understand their feelings. Although a dispute may be painful at the time, something positive can emerge from it. A conflict can serve to jolt you out of your usual standpoint and widen your horizons.

Further aspects of the situation

SIX AT THE BEGINNING
Put a stop to a conflict which has just arisen. It will be relatively easy to let the matter drop without incurring too much bad feeling. There may be some minor arguments but the overall outcome will be good.

NINE IN THE SECOND PLACE
There is no point in engaging in a conflict with someone whose position is more powerful. The odds are stacked against you. Do not allow yourself to be drawn in even if it means having to swallow your pride. The consequences of losing would affect others as well as yourself.

SIX IN THE THIRD PLACE
The tried and tested ways of doing things are best at this time. Do not be tempted to initiate new developments in order to gain recognition. You have achieved something solid and worthwhile. Be content with this and keep a low profile.

NINE IN THE FOURTH PLACE

Do not try to gain advantage for yourself by creating conflict with someone more vulnerable. If you listen to your conscience, you will realize this is wrong. In giving up the idea, you will preserve your peace of mind.

NINE IN THE FIFTH PLACE

If the conflict is to be resolved in a satisfactory fashion, justice must be seen to be done. You may well need the help of someone qualified to act as mediator, whose judgment you can trust.

NINE AT THE TOP

If you carry the conflict through to the bitter end, you will undoubtedly win. But the price of victory will be high. Others will not respect you. You will find yourself constantly under attack. Is the matter worth losing your peace of mind for?

7

The Army

'. . . I had also made it clear to the Eighth Army that "bellyaching" would not be tolerated.'

Field-Marshal Montgomery

An army needs a strong leader who understands how to gain the trust of the troops and inspire them with his vision. At the same time, he must know how to exert authority and win obedience. This means that it is up to you to take charge of your own destiny. You must marshall your resources in the most effective way. The first step is knowing exactly what it is you want to achieve. You need to feel enthusiastic about your goal, otherwise it will be hard to carry on if the going gets tough. Then you have to decide on the course of action most likely to ensure a successful outcome. Be open to new ideas. Move ahead only when you have considered the consequences of what you propose to do. Be absolutely determined to keep going until you have reached your objective. Be generous and supportive and people will cooperate with you.

If you have asked about a relationship issue, the principle remains the same. Decide what you would like the outcome to be and take the appropriate steps to achieve it. Do not act in a self-defeating way.

An opportunity for personal growth

Self-discipline is the key to dealing successfully with this situation. Refuse to be ruled by your emotions. Think of them as troops which cannot be allowed to create mayhem in your life. You, as their leader, need to be in control. In this situation, you cannot afford to be impatient or self-indulgent. Some sacrifice in the short term may be in your overall best interests. At the same time, you must not be too hard on yourself. This would only cause you to lose heart, whereas you need to develop inner strength and confidence. These are the qualities which will carry you through difficult times.

Further aspects of the situation

SIX AT THE BEGINNING
Beware of being carried away on a wave of enthusiasm. If you rush blindly ahead, the result will be chaos. Unless you exercise self-discipline, you are asking for trouble.

NINE IN THE SECOND PLACE
You can influence the situation in a very positive way. Be diplomatic and keep your goal in mind. If you are flexible you can turn whatever happens to your advantage.

SIX IN THE THIRD PLACE
Take no chances. You are not in a strong position. If you act without carefully considering the consequences, even your best efforts will accomplish nothing.

SIX IN THE FOURTH PLACE
There is no point in struggling against overwhelming odds. Hold back and do nothing for the time being.

SIX IN THE FIFTH PLACE

The problem must be dealt with. Determination, whilst essential, is in itself not enough to ensure a successful outcome. You need also to draw on all the experience and wisdom at your disposal. Do not hesitate to consult others if this would help you. Keep an open mind.

SIX AT THE TOP

Now you have achieved your aim, beware of becoming complacent. It can be only too easy to let things slide. Acknowledge those who have helped you. If you are delegating responsibilities, be realistic about the capabilities of the individuals involved. Take care not to throw away what you have gained.

8

Joining the Right Group

'Fellowship is heaven, and lack of fellowship is hell.'
William Morris

The issue concerns your relationship to a group. No matter what the particular identity of the group, its success depends on all the participants being of like mind. They must have values in common. A successful group will serve its individual members well. You must therefore feel confident that being part of the group will help you develop your own particular gifts. This, in turn, will enable you to make an ongoing contribution to the communal well-being. Where a group works in this way, its members will benefit from a spirit of mutual support and cooperation. If you are hesitating about joining a group, do not wait too long. Those already involved in it are creating bonds as a result of shared experiences. If you miss too much of this process, it will be impossible for you to integrate successfully.

An opportunity for personal growth

If you are being asked to assume the role of group leader, the *I Ching* recommends that you consult it again to discover whether you have the necessary qualities. These are honesty, dependability and staying-power. Without them, you will do more harm than good. As leader, you need a stable personality together with a strong sense of responsibility. You must be motivated by a genuine desire to serve the group's best interests. A leader must be able to stand firm in the face of pressure. Whatever your personal inclinations, you cannot show favouritism. Group members must know that they can trust your sense of fair play. The hallmark of a healthy and well-functioning group is that it respects the dignity of its individual members. The leader must have the ability to bring this about.

Further aspects of the situation

SIX AT THE BEGINNING
The only strong basis for forming relationships is complete sincerity. What matters is who you are, not what you say. If you are honest and unpretentious, then the right people will be attracted to you. The situation will turn out unexpectedly well.

SIX IN THE SECOND PLACE
If you are true to yourself under all circumstances, you will automatically attract the right friends. Do not be concerned about whether or not other people approve of you. If you allow yourself to be influenced by such considerations, you will lose your dignity and self-respect.

SIX IN THE THIRD PLACE
You are associating with the wrong people. Confiding in those who do not understand you is not beneficial. If you become too close to them, it could prevent you from developing better relationships.

SIX IN THE FOURTH PLACE
Give your allegiance to someone in an influential position who can inspire you. But do not lose your own dignity and self-respect.

NINE IN THE FIFTH PLACE
Be sincere in word and deed. The people you are meant to associate with will then be drawn to you. You will not need to run after them or use persuasive tactics. The right relationships will form quite easily and naturally.

SIX AT THE TOP
If you have missed the right moment for joining with others, you will deeply regret a lost opportunity. It does not serve you to be in an isolated position. You need to find your place within a group in order to develop your potential.

9

Exercising Restraint

```
━━━━━━━━━
━━━━━━━━━
━━━━   ━━━━
━━━━━━━━━
━━━━━━━━━
━━━━━━━━━
```

'Though the mills of God grind slowly,
yet they grind exceeding small.'
H. W. Longfellow, *Retribution*

There is a promise of ultimate success. But circumstances are such that it
is impossible for you to take significant action at this time. Be cautious. It
would be unwise to make a show of strength. Your abilities are considerable,
but your position is not yet secure enough to allow you to make a major
impact on the situation. All you can do is prepare the ground in small ways
for the changes to come. In your day-to-day affairs, pay particular attention
to detail. Use the time of waiting to make plans, gather information and
perhaps discuss possibilities with others. Do not appear to be trying to force
an outcome.

An opportunity for personal growth

You may be longing to press ahead. But you must be patient and hold your strength in check until the situation improves. Exercise self-control and take a longer-term view. Self-restraint now will pay dividends in due course. In your dealings with others a gentle and tactful approach is called for at present. This may mean that you have to put up with a certain amount of ignorance or thoughtlessness from those around you. By being tolerant, you may be able to exert a modest degree of friendly persuasion. Little by little, you will win the trust and confidence of others. At present, to have some influence in small ways is as much as you can hope for.

Further aspects of the situation

NINE AT THE BEGINNING
Although you feel ready for change, any move you try to make will be blocked. Be patient. Do not try to control events. Concentrate on dealing with your own day-to-day business.

NINE IN THE SECOND PLACE
You may feel tempted to push ahead. Do not do anything reckless. Consider how other people have dealt successfully with a similar situation. You will realize the wisdom of holding back and cooperating with others. Otherwise you risk losing your self-respect. It would not be useful for you to be drawn into a conflict.

NINE IN THE THIRD PLACE
Over-confidence in your abilities could lead you to act unwisely. You may risk trying to force matters even though circumstances are obviously against you. In the resulting conflict you would lose dignity and put yourself in a bad light.

SIX IN THE FOURTH PLACE
All that matters is to be absolutely honest and sincere. You need not be anxious. Do not let your responsibilities cause you undue stress. Although

the situation is potentially fraught with difficulties, your truthful approach will inspire respect. You will win the cooperation of others.

NINE IN THE FIFTH PLACE
A mutually supportive relationship is enriching to each person concerned. Sharing your individual resources in a cooperative effort will bring success.

NINE AT THE TOP
Achieving your aim has taken considerable, unremitting effort. Now you are recommended to stop and be content with what you have. Don't tempt fate by being ambitious for more.

10

Treading Carefully

-- --

'Tread softly: you tread on my dreams.'

W. B. Yeats

Dealing successfully with a very difficult situation depends on being well prepared. Problems will arise if you are careless or take deliberate risks. Watch your step. Think carefully before making a move. Proceed slowly but steadily. Avoid trying to do too many things at once. Do not contemplate using radical methods. Stick to the tried and tested ways. Even if you are not in a strong position, you can make progress by being ultra-careful in your dealings with others. Be courteous, even to bad-tempered or impatient people. Do not allow yourself to be irritated by others. Treat them with respect and consideration. At the same time, you must maintain your dignity and self-possession. If you are faced with misunderstandings, do not panic. Keep your head and you will find a way to resolve them.

An opportunity for personal growth

Patience is of the essence here. Do not react emotionally. Stay calm and centred. Be tactful and sensitive to the feelings of others. Do not take everything or everybody at face value. An aggressive façade might be protecting a vulnerable nature. It would therefore be best to respond to antagonism with calm good humour. Where possible, avoid confrontation. Instead, try to find a way of creating harmony. If you are the one who is feeling vulnerable, do not try to compensate by being offensive. You do not have to prove anything or be anything you are not.

Further aspects of the situation

NINE AT THE BEGINNING
Take life as it comes. Do not be demanding of others. Be content to go at your own pace. Keep things simple.

NINE IN THE SECOND PLACE
If you go about your business in a quiet and unassuming way, you will succeed in accomplishing your aim. Be independent and keep a low profile.

SIX IN THE THIRD PLACE
Do not be over-confident. At this point you do not have a clear picture of the situation. If you bite off more than you can chew you will be inviting trouble. The consequences will be more than you can handle.

NINE IN THE FOURTH PLACE
Although you have the resources to achieve your aim, you must be very careful. Take no risks. If you proceed with caution and common sense, you can turn an apparently negative situation into something better.

NINE IN THE FIFTH PLACE
Provided you stay aware of the risks involved in what you are trying to do, you will succeed. You need determination and commitment to your goal. Learn from past mistakes. Be open to new ways of approach. If you are cautious, there will be a positive outcome.

NINE AT THE TOP

Take stock of the way you have been handling the situation. If your approach has produced a positive effect, you are on the right track. You can therefore be confident of successful results if you carry on in the same way.

11

Overall Harmony

```
 ══   ══
 ══   ══
 ═══════
 ═══════
```

'All shall be well and all shall be well and all manner of things shall be well.'

Julian of Norwich

Everything is set for a period of growth. A time of peace, harmony and prosperity is indicated. This hexagram is associated with the beginning of spring when everything begins to flourish. Existing relationships will be more harmonious. New ones can be developed. Projects will thrive. Fresh beginnings are possible in all areas of life, but changes will not simply happen of their own accord. It is true that time conditions are favourable, but it is up to you to make the most of them. You must act now to lay the foundations of future success. Take full advantage of every opportunity which beckons. Use networking to further your contacts. Letting people know what you want will bring positive results. One note of caution needs to be sounded. When everything is going well, it can be tempting to sit back and let matters take care of themselves. They will not. You must keep the kettle on the boil.

An opportunity for personal growth

This is an excellent time for 'spring-cleaning' in all areas of your life. Clearing out the old makes room for the new. Let go of anything which is no longer useful to you. This applies as much to the emotional and spiritual side of life as to material possessions. Forgive long-standing hurts and resentments. Such negative emotional clutter keeps you locked into the past. Now that you have an opportunity to make great strides in your development, nothing should be allowed to hold you back. Expand your horizons by trying new activities. By developing yourself and your skills you can use this time to best advantage.

Further aspects of the situation

NINE AT THE BEGINNING
You can make your influence more widely felt. Go out into life and be prepared to accomplish something. People who have similar values and aims will be drawn to cooperate with you. Projects which benefit others will meet with particular success.

NINE IN THE SECOND PLACE
Be kind and tolerant. Even the most apparently unlikely person may have something to contribute if approached with an open mind. Do not show favouritism or allow other people to sway your judgment. Think for yourself.

NINE IN THE THIRD PLACE
Everything changes. This is a fundamental law of life. Difficulties will no doubt arise sooner or later, but there is no point in being depressed about this. What matters is to live fully in the here and now. This approach to life will give you the inner strength to handle future problems as they arise. Do not rely on people or circumstances to make you happy. Over-dependence on others will weaken your spirit.

SIX IN THE FOURTH PLACE
Cooperate with others without having ulterior motives for doing so. People will be more receptive to you if they sense you are genuine. Do not try to impress.

SIX IN THE FIFTH PLACE
Do not be arrogant. Great success is indicated provided that you are willing to be of service to others. In doing so, you will gain their support. Everybody concerned will benefit.

SIX AT THE TOP
With the end of the favourable cycle comes the beginning of the inevitable decline. Because this is part of a natural process, you can do nothing to stop it. There is no point in struggling against what you cannot change. Instead, pay attention to your responsibilities and strengthen your ties with those closest to you. Self-control is essential.

12

Stagnation

———————
———————
——— ———
——— ———

'Nothing happens, nobody comes, nobody goes, it's awful.'
Samuel Beckett, *Waiting for Godot*

The situation has reached stalemate. Too many obstacles stand in the way of further progress. Your best efforts to try and resolve matters meet with failure. It seems as though you are dogged by bad luck. Do not expect help from people who are in fact incapable of supporting you. Those who do not share your values will not be interested in your current predicament; they have their own agendas. Your views will be neither accepted nor understood. Even in hitherto good relationships, communication may now be problematic. Misunderstandings easily occur. The best course of action would be to distance yourself from the situation for the time being. Do not even try to force further developments. Be patient. In due course better times will come. In the meantime do not lose faith in yourself.

An opportunity for personal growth

However trying the situation, do not lower your standards. Stand up for what you believe to be right. Do not get involved in any situation which would mean compromising yourself. A tempting offer could, on the face of it, promise an easy way out. But do not be persuaded into making a move at this time. If enticing rewards are offered, they may well have strings attached. In the long run, the cost to your self-respect would be too high. Accept that you must rely on your own resources. The strength you gain from having to do so will stand you in good stead in the future. You could benefit from spending some time alone. This would help to counteract the pressures of a negative situation.

Further aspects of the situation

SIX AT THE BEGINNING
Unless you can exert a positive influence on the situation, do not remain involved in it. Otherwise, any attempt you make to take action will set in motion a chain of unfortunate events. It is better to distance yourself and avoid the possibility of compromising yourself.

SIX IN THE SECOND PLACE
Be tolerant but without getting involved. For the time being, be content with keeping a low profile. If you can remain independent in mind and spirit at this time, success will be yours in the longer term.

SIX IN THE THIRD PLACE
If you try to do something beyond your capabilities, you will put yourself in a humiliating position. Do not use underhand methods to try and get the results you want. Such action will backfire on you.

NINE IN THE FOURTH PLACE
The time of stagnation is drawing to a close. You will be able to play a leading role in bringing about a change to new and quite different conditions. Do not allow selfish considerations to influence your judgment. Provided that your motives are beyond reproach, the outcome will be extremely successful.

NINE IN THE FIFTH PLACE

The good times are coming. You can be instrumental in bringing about a radical change for the better. But don't assume that you are safely home and dry. There is still a possibility that things could go wrong. This can be avoided if you pay careful attention to detail. Take nothing for granted. Stand up for what you feel to be right. By making your position secure, you will be building solid foundations for your future well-being.

NINE AT THE TOP

Light appears at the end of the tunnel. The time of stagnation is ending. But change will not happen simply of its own accord. You must play an active part. When you see an opportunity to help get things moving, take it. You will have cause to celebrate.

13

Cooperating *With* Others

```
━━━━━━━━
━━━━━━━━
━━━━━━━━
━━━  ━━━
━━━━━━━━
```

'Harmony between two individuals is never granted — it has to be conquered indefinitely.'

Simone de Beauvoir

Your aim can best be achieved within the context of a group of like-minded people. They may be friends, co-workers, a political organization or spiritual group, or any other group of which you are a member. Participating in a joint effort will help you to achieve more than you could alone. The energy generated by a group of people united in a single purpose can move mountains. Give your whole-hearted support. This will help others to do the same. An atmosphere must be created which encourages each individual to make their contribution. If you are strong-minded and centred within yourself, there is scope for you to have considerable influence. When problems arise, do not lose heart. If you are open-minded and determined to succeed, solutions will occur to you. Do not hesitate to communicate these to others.

An opportunity for personal growth

The group will work well only if cliques do not form within it. If you are involved in an organizational capacity, you must try to discourage separatist attitudes. Keep your aims firmly in mind and support the efforts of the group to achieve them. Each person needs a role which will help him or her to function most effectively within the group. If individuals feel that their abilities are being used and valued, ill-feeling will be avoided. A spirit of generosity and openness will prevail. This is what will give the group its power. At the same time, it would be unrealistic to expect all concerned to form close bonds immediately. People need time and opportunity to get to know and trust each other.

Further aspects of the situation

NINE AT THE BEGINNING
A group of people with similar aims comes together. All are in agreement as to what needs to be achieved. Nobody misunderstands the position or has a hidden agenda of their own. As long as everybody involved remains committed to the same goal, all will be well.

SIX IN THE SECOND PLACE
Factions have formed within the group. Some of its members feel superior to others and have formed themselves into an exclusive clique. The potential of the group is therefore limited. Unless something is done, the group will not achieve its aims.

NINE IN THE THIRD PLACE
A conflict of interests has arisen amongst those who are meant to be working towards a common goal. The result is that people no longer trust one another. Competition has replaced cooperation. This is most unfortunate because it prevents progress being made. You must examine your aims again. It is essential that each person involved is in agreement with them.

NINE IN THE FOURTH PLACE

Misunderstandings separate you from others, leaving you on the defensive. In the end all concerned will come to their senses and realize that fighting will achieve nothing. The situation will then improve.

NINE IN THE FIFTH PLACE

The situation is distressing. You are meant to be part of a group or a partnership. Yet you are prevented from gaining access to the person or people involved. Be patient. The bonds between you are so strong that nothing can ultimately stand in your way. If you make your feelings known, you will meet with a response. Together you can work to overcome the obstacles which separate you. The result will be a joyful reunion.

NINE AT THE TOP

You can certainly gain some benefit from joining with others. But nothing of outstanding significance will be achieved.

14

Outstanding Good Fortune

'The day of fortune is like a harvest day,
We must be busy when the corn is ripe.'
Goethe

Tremendous possibilities are available to you. Projects you undertake now will be very successful. Relationships will thrive. Outstanding good fortune is indicated. This might well mean a considerable and possibly unexpected improvement in your circumstances. But it could also refer to the way in which you are now able to take charge of your life. You can make great strides in the direction of fulfilling your potential. In terms of your current situation, you are quite clear about where you stand and what you are aiming for. You are in a position to organize your life in a way which will best achieve your goal. Let your decisions and actions be based on what you sincerely believe to be right. Never compromise your truth. Be independent in your thinking, live according to your highest values and fortune will smile upon you.

An opportunity for personal growth

Whatever the situation, your position in it is centre-stage, right in the spotlight. You now have an opportunity to shine. Because you have so much to offer, whatever you would like to accomplish is possible. Do not let this to go to your head. Be kind and unselfish. If you are modest and open-minded, you will gain the respect of everybody involved. You have considerable influence so be sure to use it well. Count your blessings and appreciate them fully. You have a responsibility to all concerned, not least yourself, to maximize your resources. Provided that your motives are unselfish, you will succeed. But do be careful not to bite off more than you can chew. If you need help, don't be too proud to ask for it.

Further aspects of the situation

NINE AT THE BEGINNING
All is going well. But there has as yet been no opportunity for anything to go wrong. Do not be lulled into a false sense of security. The situation is just at its beginning and will invariably have its ups and downs. If you are careful not to invite trouble, you will meet with no major problems.

NINE IN THE SECOND PLACE
This is not a time to hide your light under a bushel. You have many gifts and abilities and are now in a position to use them to great advantage. Help is available to enable you to achieve your goals.

NINE IN THE THIRD PLACE
You are blessed with certain gifts. They are not meant to be used for yourself alone. If others benefit from your resources, you will be rewarded. Only small-minded people wish to keep everything for themselves.

NINE IN THE FOURTH PLACE

Do not be conceited. Boasting about what you have will only make others feel envious. If the result is that they try to compete with you, trouble will follow. Be modest and cooperative.

SIX IN THE FIFTH PLACE

Because you are so obviously sincere and trustworthy, people warm to you. But watch out for those who might wish to take advantage of your openness and good nature. Be discriminating about who you take into your confidence. Do not allow anybody to behave disrespectfully to you.

NINE AT THE TOP

This is a splendid line which represents great achievement. According to ancient Chinese thought, the able person who does not look for recognition will be blessed by Heaven and receive its help. This means you must be modest and not let success go to your head. Be as willing to support as to lead.

15

Modesty

'If you can talk with crowds and keep your virtue,
Or walk with kings – nor lose the common touch.'

Rudyard Kipling, *If*

Modesty is not about being shy. It means being yourself, natural and unpretentious. To have a modest attitude is to have a balanced appreciation of your own value. It is to be aware of both your strengths and your weaknesses. Dealing successfully with the current situation does not involve trying to impress or be anything you are not. On the one hand, do not be conceited. A modest person does not flaunt their achievements or their abilities. On the other hand you must not undervalue yourself. It is not a case of hiding your light under a bushel. If you have a light, then let it shine. But do not set yourself up to outshine others. Be tolerant and do not think of yourself as being more special than anybody else. Never be patronizing. Be realistic. Deal with the situation as it is rather than as you think it should be. Wishful thinking is not useful. If you have your feet on the ground, you will not easily be taken in by appearances. Do not exaggerate your feelings or make an unnecessary drama out of events.

Accept the situation with good humour and generosity of spirit. You will then attract the support you need. If you have a modest attitude, whatever you attempt will have a successful outcome.

An opportunity for personal growth

Working on your self-development will bring you good fortune at this time. The challenge lies in overcoming pride so as to recognize your shortcomings. Be prepared to accept difficulties without feeling sorry for yourself. Things cannot possibly always go the way you would like them to. Take nothing and nobody for granted. The world does not owe you anything. Do not be over-ambitious. Consider what is truly of value in the situation. Make this the priority on which you base your choices. No matter what the advantages or the drawbacks of your current circumstances, all that matters is to have a modest outlook. This will enable you to use whatever resources you have in the most creative way.

Further aspects of the situation

SIX AT THE BEGINNING
Do not be over-dramatic or concerned about making an impression on others. Quiet, steady progress is the way to success. To achieve something worthwhile, all you have to do is get on with it.

SIX IN THE SECOND PLACE
A truly modest attitude will reveal itself in everything you say and do. Others will recognize your worth. Without any effort on your part to draw attention to yourself, your influence will make itself felt. This will bring you good fortune.

NINE IN THE THIRD PLACE
Work hard towards achieving your goal. Do not look upon any aspect of the work as being beneath you. Be prepared to do whatever is necessary to carry matters through to their conclusion. You will attract the support necessary to ensure a highly successful result.

SIX IN THE FOURTH PLACE

You are in a strong position. Considerable progress is possible. Provided that you remain genuinely committed to what you are doing, people will be willing to help you.

SIX IN THE FIFTH PLACE

If you have a position of responsibility, there are times when you must be prepared to be assertive. If you were to let things drift, no further progress would be made. A calm and objective approach will ensure that you do not alienate anybody involved. Those whose help you need will then be willing to lend you their support.

SIX AT THE TOP

If you are dissatisfied with the current state of affairs, do not blame others. Exercise self-control. Consider where your own attitudes might need to change. Take responsibility for yourself and your own well-being. You can then make a considerable impact on the situation.

Note: This hexagram is unusual in that all the lines are favourable. The implication is that a truly modest attitude enables you to master any situation. This demonstrates how highly the ancient Chinese valued the quality of modesty.

16

Thinking Ahead

```
══  ══
══  ══
══  ══
```

'Forewarned, forearmed, to be prepared is half the victory.'

Cervantes

As a result of foresight and careful preparation, you can enjoy a period of comfort and relaxation. No major problems are indicated. But take care not to become lazy or over-indulgent. You must continue to create the conditions which will ensure your future well-being. With confidence and enthusiasm, you can expand your field of activity and achieve a great deal. New developments can be successfully promoted. Keep on your toes. Take advantage of any opportunity to let others know of your aims. Anticipate what you will need in order to make progress. Find people who can help you with your preparations. If you are passionately interested in achieving something, your enthusiasm will attract others and win their cooperation. Provided you go about it in the right way, those involved will be happy to follow your lead.

An opportunity for personal growth

In recommending the best way of influencing people, the ancient text takes music as a model. It notes the mysterious power of music to move and inspire people and bring them together. Because of this, music was always used in religious ceremonies. What is implied is that effective influence is a result of being in tune both with yourself and others. Being in harmony with yourself means listening to your intuition and speaking your truth. Creating harmony with other people involves putting your message across in a way they feel comfortable with. This in turn depends on understanding what it is that matters to them. If you communicate what you have to say in a way that is relevant to their own concerns, people will respond favourably.

Further aspects of the situation

SIX AT THE BEGINNING
Do not be complacent. If you flaunt your achievements or boast about people you are connected with, you will alienate others.

SIX IN THE SECOND PLACE
Take care not to get carried away by other people's enthusiasm. Do not follow anybody else's lead. Rely on your own judgment. In order to succeed, you must be as solid and reliable as a rock. Watch out for the very first signs of change in the situation. Take appropriate action immediately.

SIX IN THE THIRD PLACE
Be self-reliant and prepared to work for what you want. If you expect others to provide for your needs, you will lose opportunities which would enable you to take care of yourself.

NINE IN THE FOURTH PLACE
You know that you are on the right path. Do not hesitate to express your ideas with confidence. Others will recognize that you are sincere and will feel inspired by your optimism and positive attitude. You will have no trouble in winning the cooperation you need to fulfil your aim.

57

SIX IN THE FIFTH PLACE

You are subjected to constant pressure from which there seems to be no respite. Efforts to make progress meet with difficulties. Nevertheless, you are able to keep going.

SIX AT THE TOP

You are in danger of being carried away on the wings of fantasy. Do not delude yourself. Only by being realistic will you avoid problems.

17

Being Adaptable

‾‾ ‾ ‾
━━━━━━
‾‾ ‾ ‾
━━━━━━

'Hitch your wagon to a star.'
Ralph Waldo Emerson

Follow your conscience. Set yourself the highest standards. Make sure that what you are aiming for will truly enhance your life. Be careful about who you choose to associate with. You cannot afford to waste your time. There is so much that is worthwhile to be accomplished. Be patient if things do not seem to be moving as quickly as you would like. Adapt to the way things are rather than struggling to make them as you would like them to be. This will only exhaust you. Be open-minded and ready to learn from others. Outstanding success is indicated here but only if you are prepared to explore new possibilities. You cannot pursue a new path if at the same time you are trying to follow the old, familiar ways. This means that you must overcome your prejudices and adopt a more flexible approach to situations and to people. Widen your outlook and you will discover that the world is your oyster.

An opportunity for personal growth

Be true to your highest values, no matter what the circumstances. Your integrity will win the respect of others. This is especially important if you are in a position of influence or authority, however modest. You must learn to serve the interests of those you have responsibility for. Trying to exert power by force, or underhand methods, or by setting people against each other will create resistance to you. Rightly so, because you cannot expect the willing cooperation of others if you behave badly. Whereas if people know you can be trusted to do what is right, they will be happy to follow your lead. The same principle applies in situations where your role is to follow somebody else. You will want to feel confident that the leader has your best interests at heart.

Further aspects of the situation

NINE AT THE BEGINNING
You need a wider viewpoint. Listen to the views of others and be open to the possibility of learning something new. Use your discrimination to decide what you can accept and what you must reject.

SIX IN THE SECOND PLACE
Taking the easy way out will be totally unproductive. If you make no effort to develop your potential, you will miss out on opportunities for success. Likewise, if you associate with people who have nothing to offer, you will lose out on more worthwhile relationships. People will judge you by the company you keep. Put a higher value on yourself.

SIX IN THE THIRD PLACE
If you are to succeed, you must act in your own best interests. This will involve letting go of relationships which, although familiar, are no longer right for you. However difficult this is, you must be firm. You need to pave the way for meeting people with whom you can have relationships of an altogether higher quality.

NINE IN THE FOURTH PLACE

Be sincere. Do not be taken in by flattery. And do not even think of flattering others as a way of currying favour with them. Stick to your principles and let truth be your guide. You will easily see through people who have wormed their way into your affections for their own ulterior motives.

NINE IN THE FIFTH PLACE

Aim high. Do not settle for anything second-best or mediocre. If you sincerely want the best, you will get it.

SIX AT THE TOP

Spiritual well-being is more important to you than material wealth and status. Your wish to develop yourself means that you will receive the guidance you need. As a result of the wisdom you acquire during this process, others will look to you for help and advice.

18

Dealing With Decay

'A man should never be ashamed to own he has been in the wrong, which is but saying, in other words, that he is wiser today than he was yesterday.'

Alexander Pope

Things have been going wrong for some time. Inertia on your part has meant that the situation has simply drifted along in its own way. By not taking decisive action, you have lost control of events. Matters are now thoroughly out of hand. However, the situation can be transformed. If you are prepared to pay serious attention to what has been neglected, you can repair the damage. Then you can start a new chapter in your life. But you must proceed with the utmost sensitivity and caution. Begin by considering how you have come to be in this position. This may involve unresolved issues in your background or your current environment, or both. Or perhaps you have been careless where attention to detail was essential. Insight into how the problem has been caused will help you to identify the most appropriate way to remedy it. Be determined to take constructive action. If you persevere, the outcome will be highly successful.

An opportunity for personal growth

You have been unable to fulfil your potential. But your commitment to working on the problems involved will pave the way to a far more satisfying situation. Be patient. Considerable effort may be needed. Things which have gone wrong in the past can take time to put right. Notice where negative attitudes or patterns of behaviour have been holding you back. With determination, and perhaps some help, you can change them. You now have the opportunity to make amends for past wrongs. The way forward is through forgiveness. Continuing to blame yourself or others will achieve nothing. Whereas by forgiving, you can free yourself from the destructive effects of the past and begin to create your own well-being. Once you accept responsibility for yourself, your self-respect will benefit hugely.

Further aspects of the situation

SIX AT THE BEGINNING
Doing the expected thing has prevented you from being as effective as you might be. Traditional ways are by their nature resistant to change. But if you proceed very cautiously, with great awareness, your efforts will meet with success.

NINE IN THE SECOND PLACE
Past mistakes must now be resolved. You must approach the matter with gentleness and sensitivity so as not to tread on the feelings of others.

NINE IN THE THIRD PLACE
You are keen to put the effects of past mistakes behind you so that you are free to move forward. You are right to do so. Your energetic and assertive approach will meet with some resistance from others. But in the end no great harm will be done.

SIX IN THE FOURTH PLACE
Lack of action over a period of time has caused the situation to deteriorate. Further indecision and weakness on your part will only serve to make

matters worse. Carrying on in this way will have a disastrous effect on your self-confidence.

SIX IN THE FIFTH PLACE

You are faced with the results of a long-standing problem. If you are willing to take responsibility for putting things right, others will be only too happy to support you. Everybody concerned will appreciate your efforts.

NINE AT THE TOP

Your concern is with the spiritual rather than the material side of life. Worldly ambition, money and status are not a priority at this time. This does not mean that you are lazy or uncaring. On the contrary, your sincere efforts at self-development are a step in the direction of transforming the world for the better. Each individual who tries to discover their true worth, as opposed to their market value, introduces a little more light into a greedy, over-materialistic culture.

19

Moving Towards
Your Goal

'I dreamed that, as I wandered by the way,
Bare Winter suddenly was changed to Spring.'
                              Percy Bysshe Shelley

It is as though spring is in the air. You can look forward with certainty to a time when your affairs will blossom. But a natural process of growth is at work. It cannot be hurried. Steps remain to be taken. Although success is inevitable, nothing will be resolved immediately. Opportunities beckon which will involve making changes. Be positive about this. Try to take an all-round view of matters, especially where relationships are involved. Consider the effect of such changes on other people. Make their well-being a priority as you decide what to do. If you hold a position of authority, however modest, you will have a good deal of influence at this time. Use it well by helping and encouraging those for whom you are responsible. Where it is appropriate to delegate, do so. The positive feedback you receive will be very good for your own self-confidence and optimism.

An opportunity for personal growth

Do not allow yourself to become too comfortable just because things are beginning to go well. This is indeed the start of a period of growth. But do not assume that you can simply sit back and let things happen. You must play your part in nurturing the situation so that long-term success is assured. Work hard to take maximum advantage of the opportunities offered. Keep on top of things in order to notice the smallest signs of deterioration. Any potential problem must be nipped in the bud. In your relationships, pay attention to the needs of others. This favourable time will not last indefinitely. But if you establish strong foundations now, you will move safely through more difficult times in the future.

Further aspects of the situation

NINE AT THE BEGINNING
Cooperating with others will put you in a stronger position. Be determined to do what you feel is right.

NINE IN THE SECOND PLACE
The balance is about to swing in your favour. The efforts you have made are beginning to show results. Go ahead with whatever you have in mind. You will get the support you need.

SIX IN THE THIRD PLACE
Everything is going well. But you must keep your long-term goal in mind, otherwise there is the risk of becoming careless and over-confident. Take great care not to waste the resources you currently have at your disposal. This would create problems in the longer term.

SIX IN THE FOURTH PLACE
Your approach is absolutely correct. You know just what to do and should act accordingly.

SIX IN THE FIFTH PLACE
Make sure that you are as fully informed about the situation as possible. This will ensure that the action you take will be the most beneficial to all concerned. Choose competent helpers whose aims are compatible with yours.

SIX AT THE TOP
You have a wealth of experience to offer. Be prepared to share it generously with others. Your involvement will be of immense benefit to all concerned.

20

Taking an Overview

_____
_____
__ __
__ __
__ __

'He is a great observer, and he looks
Quite through the deeds of men.'
Shakespeare, _Julius Caesar_

Take a completely fresh look at the situation. No matter what others
may say or do, put yourself in the position of a detached observer. Be
open-minded, unemotional and ready to learn. Taking an overview will help
you to appreciate how the current state of affairs has come about. Gradually
you will acquire a deeper understanding of what is involved. It will become
clear to you what the end result will be if matters carry on developing in this
way. Because your ideas make sense, others will be prepared to listen. They
will appreciate that your views are fair and well-balanced. Act with integrity
to yourself. Use your knowledge to benefit others not to manipulate the
situation for your own ends.

An opportunity for personal growth

As your understanding of the situation grows, it must be translated into action. Fresh insights are essential but can only be of benefit once they are incorporated into your life. Old attitudes must change. Learning not to take things too personally is a major lesson at this time. This means that your approach to people and events will be based on a wider perspective than usual. As a result you will not be easily fooled. At the same time you will become more tolerant of others and their mistakes. The overall effect will be that your influence on the situation will grow without any effort on your part. Others will be receptive to your vision and your clear understanding.

Further aspects of the situation

SIX AT THE BEGINNING
You have little understanding of the situation. You relate everything back to yourself and how it affects you personally. This attitude might be expected of a child. But for an adult it is regrettable. You must be more open-minded and develop a wider perspective.

SIX IN THE SECOND PLACE
Your current outlook is much too limited. You need to be more curious about life beyond your own narrow sphere of existence. Otherwise you cannot hope to understand another person's motives. Broaden your outlook by trying to imagine what life is like from other people's point of view.

SIX IN THE THIRD PLACE
Get to know yourself better. Do this not by becoming self-absorbed but by learning to be more objective about yourself. Be aware of how the choices you make affect your environment. Receiving positive feedback indicates that are on the right track. Whereas if matters are deteriorating, it is a sign that you need to change your approach.

SIX IN THE FOURTH PLACE

Your current experience is providing an opportunity to expand your horizons. Your ability to see the wider picture will give you considerable influence in the situation.

NINE IN THE FIFTH PLACE

If you are in a position of influence over others, you must take your responsibilities seriously. It is up to you to set an example. You will know if you are succeeding by observing the effect you are having on those involved. If you can see positive results, you can safely assume that your influence is beneficial.

NINE AT THE TOP

The best position of all is that of being unconcerned with personal ambition. If you are not motivated by self-interest you have the precious gift of true inner freedom. Without any effort on your part, your influence on the situation will make itself felt.

21

Getting Down to Essentials

```
━━━━━  ━━ ━━
━━━━━  ━━ ━━
━━━━━  ━━ ━━
```

'That truth lies somewhere, if we knew but where.'
William Cowper

In the ancient text, this hexagram represented legal issues. It may indeed literally mean that legal action is unavoidable. More often, however, it indicates the need to take a firm stand. Take the bull by the horns. There is no point in dithering. You must cut through to the bare bones of the situation and see what it is that really matters. All other considerations are irrelevant. Deal first and foremost with essentials. Whatever is undermining you must be identified and tackled with determination. If someone is taking advantage of you or holding you back in some respect, you must take decisive action. There can be no half measures. The problem will not disappear of its own accord. In tackling it, however, do not be too hasty or overly aggressive. On the other hand, an attitude which is too gentle and understanding would be ineffective. A successful outcome will be the result of an approach which is firm yet reasonable.

An opportunity for personal growth

If something in your current situation is not working for you, lose no time in finding out why. A negative attitude of your own might be a contributory factor. In this case, it is up to you to change it. There is little point in being your own worst enemy. Or it may be that somebody else is trying to undermine you. Once you have identified the problem, it is a case of finding the most appropriate way to counteract it. This will involve direct confrontation. Be courageous. Do not procrastinate. No compromise is possible. If you are the subject of an injustice, it is up to you to change matters.

Further aspects of the situation

NINE AT THE BEGINNING
Aggressive or stubborn attitudes must be firmly kept in check. This may apply to yourself or to others you are responsible for, particularly children. Destructive tendencies need correcting as soon as they appear. This prevents them from getting out of hand and causing serious trouble.

SIX IN THE SECOND PLACE
Have the courage to support what you know to be right. You may be concerned that your reactions are unusually strong or that you are being too hard. Do not worry. Your feelings are justified. When somebody deliberately continues to cause trouble, they must be taught a lesson.

SIX IN THE THIRD PLACE
The issue is a long-standing one. You do not have the power or authority which would enable you to deal with it. If you try to do so, you will meet with resentment. You may feel somewhat humiliated because you are unable to take effective action. Yet you cannot be blamed for trying.

NINE IN THE FOURTH PLACE

You face a difficult task. Persevere. To achieve your aim, you need a positive attitude coupled with ruthless determination. It is as though you have to chew through something tough. To succeed, you must deal with one morsel at a time until you have come to the end.

SIX IN THE FIFTH PLACE

The issue is clear-cut. You would like to be lenient. But you must balance your own personal preference with what is appropriate to the situation. You have a responsibility to be impartial and objective. This will ensure a fortunate outcome.

NINE AT THE TOP

Someone – and it could be yourself – simply will not learn. This person refuses to recognize that what they are doing is wrong. Nor do they pay the slightest attention when warned about their behaviour. They ignore good advice and continue to invite trouble. The end result can only be misfortune.

22

Adornment

'If you get simple beauty and naught else,
You get about the best thing God invents.'
Robert Browning

You can influence the situation only in small ways. Use tact and charm.
Present yourself in the best possible light. Make the most of your assets and
your abilities. You may want to make minor changes in your environment
so that it more accurately reflects your personality and your tastes. But keep
your priorities straight. Do not be conceited or self-indulgent. If you do not
value yourself as you are, no amount of material possessions or designer
clothes will help to give you a sense of worth. Remember that true beauty, like
true happiness, comes from within. An attractive appearance is of little value
if it merely disguises a selfish nature. The most elegant surroundings in the
world will not bring joy if their owners live in an atmosphere of ill-will.

An opportunity for personal growth

Each of us projects an image of how we would like to be seen by others. The psychologist Carl Jung called this the persona. A charming and attractive persona is unquestionably a great asset. But it is only one aspect of you, not the whole picture. If you are so involved with your image that you neglect your self-development, your life will become meaningless and superficial.

The consequences of putting too much value on appearances are the subject of the novel by Oscar Wilde, *The Picture of Dorian Gray*. Here the main character manages to preserve his youthful beauty for many years. But he fails to develop any strength of character in the meantime. When his outer mask finally drops away, no trace of physical beauty remains in this once-exquisite face, now ravaged by time and self-indulgence.

Further aspects of the situation

NINE AT THE BEGINNING
Use your own resources to help you make progress. Be prepared to make an effort to do whatever is necessary. Do not try to take short cuts.

SIX IN THE SECOND PLACE
Do not judge by appearances. Unless a decorative appearance is an outward sign of inner beauty, it is merely shallow and superficial. What matters now is not the outward form but the underlying worth.

NINE IN THE THIRD PLACE
When everything is going relatively well, take care not to become lazy or neglect your responsibilities. Do not lose sight of your goals.

SIX IN THE FOURTH PLACE
Honesty and simplicity are what matter most now. Deep and true friendship with someone loyal and trustworthy is far more important than chasing after the glittering prizes of life.

SIX IN THE FIFTH PLACE

All that matters is to be sincere. Your material resources may not be extensive but it is who you are that counts. Others will recognize your true worth.

NINE AT THE TOP

Be simple and straightforward in all you say and do. You have no need to hide, pretend or put on a show. Just be true to yourself, let your value speak for itself and everything will happen in exactly the right way.

23

Doing Away With the Old

$$\overline{}\ \ \overline{}$$
$$\overline{}\ \ \overline{}$$
$$\overline{}\ \ \overline{}$$

'The old order changeth, yielding place to new,
And God fulfils himself in many ways.'
Alfred, Lord Tennyson, *The Passing of Arthur*

The situation is deteriorating. Things are collapsing around you. This is a matter of external conditions beyond your control. It is not a result of your having done anything wrong. What it means is that some aspect of your life which has until now been important no longer serves your best interests. It belongs to the cycle which is coming to an end. Because a new situation needs to come into being, the old has to die. Trying to struggle against the odds would therefore be pointless. Avoid confrontation. The consequences could be devastating. There is simply too much going against you. Try to stay detached. You are already vulnerable. Emotional involvement will only weaken you further. Whereas by remaining cool and disinterested, you will give nobody the opportunity to undermine you. Keep a low profile and bide your time. Take comfort from the fact that the current process is unavoidable, if painful. It has to run its course before conditions can take a turn for the better.

An opportunity for personal growth

As there is no action you can take to improve matters, use this time to replenish your energies. In due course, you will need firm foundations on which to build the new situation. You can begin creating them now. Start building up your strength. Do not allow yourself to become depressed. Avoid any tendency to cling to the past. You can only go forward from here. Try not to have expectations of others. Take no part in power struggles. Do nothing which would compromise your sense of your own worth. Be patient. Resist any pressure to try and make things happen. Wherever possible, be kind and generous. The attitude which will best serve you is what the Chinese call *wu wei*. It means 'going with the flow' and involves trusting that matters will work themselves out as they are meant to without your having to intervene.

Further aspects of the situation

SIX AT THE BEGINNING
Someone or something is working to undermine your position. Since this involves people you think you can rely on, you must be very cautious. At this point, there is nothing you can do except be on your guard and wait until the situation becomes clearer.

SIX IN THE SECOND PLACE
You are in a difficult position and must be careful. Do not be stubborn. Distance yourself from unsupportive people. You have nothing to gain by remaining in a situation which does not serve your best interests.

SIX IN THE THIRD PLACE
Circumstances are such that you are unavoidably involved in a negative situation. Stick to your principles. Honour your own values and do nothing which would go against your conscience. If others choose to behave in a

despicable manner, that is their affair. By refusing to identify yourself with them, you can at least retain your own light and integrity.

SIX IN THE FOURTH PLACE
You are faced with misfortune and can do nothing to avoid it. Matters have gone too far for you to be able to turn back the tide of events.

SIX IN THE FIFTH PLACE
An unfavourable situation is now beginning to change for the better. Those who have been at odds with each other decide to cooperate for their mutual benefit. Success now becomes possible.

NINE AT THE TOP
The situation has deteriorated as far as it can. Now the stage is set for you to embark upon a period of renewed life, hope and personal effectiveness. Surviving a very difficult time has given you great resilience. Your future success will be a direct result of the strength you acquired in the process of battling with negative forces. This illustrates the truth that evil can only survive when fed by the power of the good. If left to feed on itself, it will use up its resources and destroy itself.

24

The Turning Point

```
═══  ═══
═══  ═══
═══  ═══
═══  ═══
═══  ═══
═════════
```

'To every thing there is a season, and a time to every purpose under
the heaven.'

Ecclesiastes

A new cycle is about to begin. After a period of stagnation or confusion,
the tide is now turning. The situation will unfold in its own way. Don't try
to force developments. Your position is not yet strong enough for you to
push ahead. The turning point is linked with the month of the winter solstice
when the new light is born again after the darkness of winter. All movement,
the hexagram tells us, is accomplished in six stages and the seventh brings
return — seven being a symbol for a complete period of time. Underlying
all natural change is a consistent rhythm: as night comes to an end, light
returns with the dawn; winter draws to its close and we know spring is near.
All that you need do is tune in to this natural rhythm as it manifests in your
own life. Right now, this means relaxing and conserving your energies.

An opportunity for personal growth

After a difficult time, you begin to experience renewed energy and optimism. Fresh possibilities beckon. You may feel ready to take action. But this would be premature. Be patient. Take time to reflect on the cycle now ending. Difficulties arose because you were not being true to yourself. Your actions and the choices you made were based on a negative point of view. In other words, your own attitudes helped to create the problems. What matters most now is to believe in yourself. Understanding this is the key to your future well-being. Then you can make a fresh start with every chance of success. New relationships are indicated, or new levels of closeness and understanding in existing relationships.

Further aspects of the situation

NINE AT THE BEGINNING
If you are contemplating a slightly dubious course of action, go no further. Do only what your conscience tells you is right. No other consideration should influence you. If you act from the right motives, everything will turn out very well.

SIX IN THE SECOND PLACE
Listen and learn from others whose views you respect. This will strengthen your own insights and help you make the right decisions.

SIX IN THE THIRD PLACE
The grass may look greener elsewhere. But in your heart you know which way you must go. Don't be tempted to abandon your chosen path. Learn to persevere.

SIX IN THE FOURTH PLACE
You have outgrown the people around you. Don't force yourself to try and fit in with them. Stand up for what you believe to be right. It is best to be true to yourself even if this means being alone for a while. Inner freedom and independence are too precious to be compromised.

81

SIX IN THE FIFTH PLACE
You realize that a new beginning is called for. Don't waste time regretting the past. All that matters is that you have now made the right decision.

SIX AT THE TOP
You have obstinately insisted on going your own way – down quite the wrong path. Now you have missed the right moment to make a change for the better. Any move you try to make will only make matters worse. All you can do is wait patiently until a new opportunity becomes available.

25

Innocence
(Avoiding Complications)

———
———
—— ——
—— ——
———

'Blessed are the pure in heart: for they shall see God.'
Matthew 5

Being innocent is quite different from being naïve or unaware of what is involved. On the contrary it means knowing what the choices are and opting to do the right thing for its own sake. INNOCENCE implies acting spontaneously, without self-interested ulterior motives. This is what will ensure a most successful outcome. Whereas if you start trying to work out how to turn the situation to your own advantage, the result will simply be confusion. Do not be too concerned about yourself. Unselfish behaviour will bring its own rewards in due course. Resist being pressured into saying or doing anything you might be ashamed of. Refuse to be involved in deception of any kind. Do nothing which might harm another. Try not to be influenced by other people's reactions. Trust your own perceptions and be guided by them. Do not compare yourself to others. Enjoy being your natural, unique self. Then you cannot fail to deal with matters in the most creative, original and appropriate way.

An opportunity for personal growth

How far are you willing to let go of control and to trust? If the outcome is to be successful, you must allow the situation to unfold naturally. Events are developing as they need to. Keep out of the way. Accept other people as they are. Do not try to force them to fit in with your expectations. Better still, do not have expectations in the first place. Live in the here and now. There is no point in trying to work everything out in advance. You cannot possibly plan for every eventuality. Situations are bound to arise which are beyond your control. The answer is to be adventurous and open to the unexpected. It is true that unforeseen events will sometimes be distressing. This cannot be helped. But if you accept them as part of the process of life, the disagreeable effects will soon pass. If you have an open mind, such events may even provide unexpected opportunities.

Further aspects of the situation

NINE IN THE FIRST PLACE
If your intentions are sincere, whatever move you make will be the right one. Follow the dictates of your heart and be spontaneous.

SIX IN THE SECOND PLACE
Dreaming about future success will not help you to achieve your aim. Be practical. Bring yourself into the here and now. Work steadily towards your goal one step at a time. Don't keep stopping to check up on your progress.

SIX IN THE THIRD PLACE
Life is not always fair. There are times when difficulties arise through no fault of your own. Do not allow such unexpected problems to make you bitter or cynical. Taking matters personally will only weaken your position further. Be philosophical.

84

NINE IN THE FOURTH PLACE

You must stick to what you feel is right. Resist any pressure to change course. Do not feel obliged to comply with other people's wishes.

NINE IN THE FIFTH PLACE

An unexpected difficulty will resolve itself of its own accord. There is nothing you need do about it. In due course all will be well again. The less you try to intervene, the better.

NINE AT THE TOP

You have done as much as you can. Any further action would be a mistake. However good your intentions, you would be misunderstood.

26

Controlling Your
Resources

$$\begin{array}{c} \underline{\hspace{4em}} \\[-0.3em] \underline{\hspace{1.5em}}\ \ \underline{\hspace{1.5em}} \\[-0.3em] \underline{\hspace{1.5em}}\ \ \underline{\hspace{1.5em}} \\[-0.3em] \underline{\hspace{4em}} \\[-0.3em] \underline{\hspace{4em}} \end{array}$$

'. . . one must have the courage to dare.'
Dostoevsky, *Crime and Punishment*

A great deal is possible now. If you take the first steps, doors will
begin to open for you. Identify all the resources you have at your
disposal. You may have accumulated money, friends, knowledge, experience,
particular abilities or qualities – the possibilities are endless. These are
your assets. Now is the time to capitalize on them. Decide how you
can best use them in order to accomplish your aims. If you have
been putting off something which needs doing, get going. If you need
information, gather it. Once you have made adequate preparations,
take action. Do not hesitate to enlist the help you need. Be very
productive. Stretch yourself beyond your current limits. Give the best
of which you are capable. Be determined to make the most of each
moment of each day. Once you have put your plans into action you

must keep on top of things. If you are careless, you risk losing your momentum.

An opportunity for personal growth

However enthusiastic you feel, do not be impatient. Success depends on how well you control the resources at your disposal. Before rushing headlong into something, stop and consider the consequences. Learn to pace yourself. Stay focused on your aims. Organize your activities around achieving them. Do not allow yourself to be distracted by irrelevant issues. You must not fritter away time or assets. Do not hesitate to offer your services to others. You can make a significant contribution to your environment at this time. Make your presence felt. Keeping a low profile is not appropriate right now. If you have been holding back from involvement with a person or situation, drop your inhibitions. The more you give of yourself, the more energy you will generate.

Further aspects of the situation

NINE AT THE BEGINNING
You would like to push ahead but the time is not right. There are obstacles in the way. If you try to force matters you will invite trouble. Wait calmly until an appropriate outlet for your energy is offered.

NINE IN THE SECOND PLACE
You are held back by circumstances beyond your control. Exercise self-restraint. Stay centred and do not lose sight of your goal.

NINE IN THE THIRD PLACE
Be careful. Do not rush ahead. The way to move towards your goal is one step at a time.

SIX IN THE FOURTH PLACE
Be extremely careful not to dissipate your resources before the time is ripe. Hold back. By thinking ahead you can anticipate difficulties. Take action

now to prevent them becoming a reality. Your caution will be rewarded by a highly successful outcome.

SIX IN THE FIFTH PLACE
Matters threaten to get out of hand. You must take action to prevent this. Avoid point-blank confrontation. An indirect approach will be far more effective. Look for the underlying cause of the disturbance. To deal with this is to remove the sting from the situation. There will be no further trouble.

NINE AT THE TOP
The resources you have steadily accumulated can at last be used. You can now achieve something truly worthwhile. Nothing holds you back from achieving your aims and enjoying great success.

27

Nourishing

```
━━━━━━━━━━
━━━  ━━━
━━━  ━━━
━━━  ━━━
━━━━━━━━━━
```

'. . . for whatsoever a man soweth, that shall he also reap.'
St. Paul's Epistle to the Galatians

The issue here is one of providing nourishment either for yourself or others. This may literally involve the kind of food you eat but can apply equally to emotional and spiritual nourishment. What you allow into your mind is just as important as what you put into your body. Every day you make choices concerning what food to take into your body and what information to take into your mind. Use your discrimination as to what is wholesome and nourishing and what is not. A regular diet of junk food and violent movies is unlikely to lead to either a healthy body or a balanced and peaceful state of mind. Respect yourself enough to take proper care of yourself. And be careful about who you choose to give your care to. Do not throw your pearls before swine. Be wary of lavishing care and attention on people who refuse to look after themselves properly.

An opportunity for personal growth

Your physical health is affected by what and how you eat. When you feel calm and well-balanced, the tendency is to eat no more than you need of good, wholesome food. In the same way, your mental well-being depends on the nature of the thoughts which occupy your mind. Negative attitudes serve only to make you miserable. And if you expect things to go wrong, they quite often do. Whereas if you cultivate a positive outlook, all aspects of your life will improve. It is a matter of choice and self-control. Your state of mind also influences the way you communicate with others. Words spoken in temper, for instance, cannot be taken back and may be very destructive. Whereas if your mind is at peace, what you have to say will benefit others and nurture your relationships.

Further aspects of the situation

NINE AT THE BEGINNING
Envying those who have more than you is not only a waste of time but gradually eats away at your own self-respect. Stop comparing yourself with others. Make the best of your own resources. Learn to appreciate what you do have and you will feel more at peace with yourself.

SIX IN THE SECOND PLACE
Be willing to take care of your own needs. The world does not owe you a living. Do not expect others to do for you what you are capable of doing for yourself. Stick to what is within your capabilities and do not be ambitious for more.

SIX IN THE THIRD PLACE
You are trying to nourish yourself from the wrong sources. This might apply to the food you eat, the company you keep or the way you use your leisure. Unless this changes, you will gradually deplete your energy. The end result will be unfortunate.

SIX IN THE FOURTH PLACE
You are in a position to be of benefit to others but cannot do this alone.
Be on the look-out for people who can help you.

SIX IN THE FIFTH PLACE
Although you would like to help others, you lack the necessary abilities and
should not attempt to do so alone. Turn your attention to finding somebody
who has the knowledge and experience to help you.

NINE AT THE TOP
You can be of great benefit to others. This position brings with it serious
responsibilities. Provided you are aware of these, you will successfully
accomplish something quite difficult.

28

Overload

```
___  _  ___
_____
_____
_____
_____
___  _  ___
```

'The world is too much with us; late and soon,
Getting and spending, we lay waste our powers:'
William Wordsworth

The situation has reached crisis point. You are under such great pressure
that something has to give. To lighten the load you are carrying, you must
take prompt action, but nothing can be forced. You cannot know what to do
for the best without first understanding the underlying cause of the problem.
There is a distinct lack of balance in this situation. Your own attitudes may
be at fault in that they may be too one-sided or obsessive. You could be
too aggressive, for example, too fearful – or even too determined to do
something for which you do not have the appropriate gifts or skills. The
source of stress could also lie within a relationship. Somebody may be
exaggerating their feelings or behaving in an unacceptable way. But no
matter what the particular issue, serious adjustments have to be made so
as to redress the balance.

An opportunity for personal growth

Stop trying to meet all the demands made on you, whether they are made by others or are self-imposed. It makes life far too confusing and complicated. You must sort out your priorities. What do you really want to happen? Where do your true responsibilities lie? Look at all the factors involved. Consider everything which claims your time and attention. Once you know what your aim is, you can begin to organize your life around it. Inevitably this will mean giving up something. But you must be firm and protect your own best interests, even if this means having to go it alone. If you can find the courage to make the necessary changes, success is assured.

Further aspects of the situation

SIX AT THE BEGINNING
Be extremely careful. A successful outcome depends on paying great attention to detail at the beginning. Your planning must be meticulous.

NINE IN THE SECOND PLACE
Strange or unexpected developments bring new life into the situation. Unusual partnerships are favoured and off-beat ways of dealing with things.

NINE IN THE THIRD PLACE
Beware of being stubborn and arrogant. If you refuse to cooperate with others and insist on pushing ahead on your own, you will isolate yourself. This would be extremely unfortunate.

NINE IN THE FOURTH PLACE
Because you enjoy a great deal of support, you are now in a position of strength. If you use your abilities to help others, matters will go very well. But if you are greedy and misuse your resources for your own ends, you will be the loser in the end.

NINE IN THE FIFTH PLACE
Face facts now. If you wait too long before taking action, the situation will go beyond the point where you can make a difference. Get to the root of the matter. Otherwise even your best efforts to put things right will produce no results.

SIX AT THE TOP
To have any hope of success means taking huge risks. Something will have to be sacrificed. Only you can decide if the price is worth paying. Nobody has the right to judge you.

29

Danger (The Abyss)

```
━━━━   ━━  ━━
━━━━━━━━━━━━
━━━━   ━━  ━━
━━━━━━━━━━━━
━━━━━━━━━━━━
━━━━   ━━  ━━
```

'But screw your courage to the sticking place,
And we'll not fail.'

Shakespeare, *Macbeth*

The situation is fraught with difficulties. You have to face the fact that
they will not simply go away. All you can do is grit your teeth and rise
to the challenge. Begin by accepting the reality of the situation just as it
is. Wishful thinking is useless. Believe in yourself and refuse to give up,
however bad things may seem. Be true to yourself and stand up for what
you know to be right. Do not be concerned with whether others approve
or not. All this takes courage. However, you will be rewarded by a much
deeper insight into the issues involved. Armed with this knowledge, you will
begin to understand what to do for the best.

An opportunity for personal growth

You face a test of your patience and determination. However difficult the situation, you must refuse to become a victim of circumstances. Do not allow your emotions to rule you. To give up at this stage would be the worst thing possible. Like water which flows without stopping through an abyss, you must carry on regardless of the obstacles which face you. Refuse to be paralysed by feelings of depression or despair. This would be like being trapped in the abyss. Live each day as it comes and try to stay calm. Keeping a cool head will help you to handle moments of crisis. It may seem that you are having to persevere against overwhelming odds. But if you can keep going, your efforts will eventually be crowned with success.

Further aspects of the situation

SIX AT THE BEGINNING
Because you have over-estimated your ability to handle the situation, you are now in a hazardous position. Yet you are reluctant to extricate yourself. Perhaps you do not appreciate just how serious things have become. You are in danger of growing so used to your condition that you cannot see how badly it is affecting you.

NINE IN THE SECOND PLACE
You can have only a very limited effect on the situation at this time. Although you realize that change is necessary, what exactly you can do about it is not yet clear. Be patient and do what you can in small ways. Take one cautious step at a time.

SIX IN THE THIRD PLACE
Anything you try to do now will only make the situation worse. It's as though you are stuck in a hole, desperately trying to find a way out. But you succeed only in digging yourself in even deeper. The answer is to stop struggling and wait. If you can remain calm, the solution will eventually reveal itself.

SIX IN THE FOURTH PLACE
Be honest and straightforward. You may be concerned that what you have to offer is inadequate, but because you genuinely want to make a contribution, it will be accepted. Others will recognize that you are sincere. This is all that matters.

NINE IN THE FIFTH PLACE
You have gone as far as circumstances will allow. Be content with what you have achieved and do not try to do more. Being too ambitious at this time will create further difficulties.

SIX AT THE TOP
No good at all will come of insisting on having your own way. Your obstinacy prevents you from seeing that you are on quite the wrong track. Until you understand that your behaviour is self-defeating, the situation cannot improve.

30

Shedding Light on Things

———————
—— ——
———————
———————
—— ——
———————

'More light!'
Goethe

It is up to you to shed some light on the situation. You can only do so if you are clear in your own mind as to what is going on. To arrive at this point you will need a degree of detachment. Do not take personally anything others may say or do. If you get caught up in emotional issues or power struggles you will have no hope of seeing the whole picture. If you want to handle matters in the most intelligent way, the key word is acceptance. Do not be anxious or pessimistic. Rather than struggling against circumstances or burying your head in the sand, accept that whatever is happening is for the best. Examine the issues involved with an open mind. Notice where improvement is possible. Exploring the positive aspects of the situation will not only be to your own advantage. It will also benefit everybody involved.

An opportunity for personal growth

Acceptance is the great lesson of this situation. This does not mean simply putting up with things. What it does involve is facing all the facts. The more willing you are to accept the reality of the matter, the better your chances of seeing the whole picture. This will lead you to the truth about what is happening. Once you have a clear and unprejudiced view of things, you cannot be taken in or side-tracked by irrelevant considerations. The way to handle the issue will then become clear. On the other hand, if you simply react emotionally to the situation, your views will be very one-sided. In that state of mind you are unlikely to act in the most constructive way.

Further aspects of the situation

NINE AT THE BEGINNING
To ensure the best possible outcome, you must make the best possible start. At the beginning of anything, there is likely to be confusion. This must be sorted out before it can develop and take hold of the situation. Go slowly and carefully, paying attention to detail. Think before you make a move. Have you made all the necessary preparations for taking this step?

SIX IN THE SECOND PLACE
If you can maintain a balanced attitude, you are guaranteed great success. Keep calm and stay in control of yourself. Do not go to extremes in any way. Be open-minded and positive.

NINE IN THE THIRD PLACE
Accept fate. Do not waste time regretting the past or worrying about the future. Be responsible for living as fully as possible in the here and now. Take advantage of the opportunities which are available to you. If you let things slide, you will come to regret it.

NINE IN THE FOURTH PLACE
You are in too much of a hurry. This is not the way to create something of lasting value. If you do not slow down you risk burning yourself out.

SIX IN THE FIFTH PLACE

As you begin to understand the situation more clearly, you realize that you cannot avoid giving up or coming to terms with something. Feelings of sadness are almost inevitable – but they will pass. In your heart, you know you have no choice but to accept the reality. The changes you must make will lead to a much better situation.

NINE AT THE TOP

A clear mind will enable you to find the source of the difficulty. If other people are involved, do the minimum necessary to deal with the matter. Do not make it into a major issue. If problems have arisen because of your refusal to accept reality, aim for a more balanced attitude. Avoid being over-dramatic or too hard on yourself. Just deal with things as best you can.

31

Mutual Attraction

― ――
――――
―――― ―
― ―

'Love goes towards love, as schoolboys from their books;'
Shakespeare, *Romeo and Juliet*

What is represented is a situation where you are attracted to someone with whom you want to form a relationship. This is not necessarily a question of a love affair. It can refer to any area of your life which involves connecting with others in order to create a mutually beneficial relationship. Falling in love is an obvious example. But it can apply equally to other types of friendship and to family or business relationships. The real issue is how you interact with whoever else is involved. Relationships thrive on care and attention. An aggressive approach would be quite wrong. Be patient and considerate. Do not try to force the pace. Attraction between people is not something which can be controlled. It can only be allowed to develop in its own way. Over time, you will meet and communicate at a deeper level. Strong bonds will be forged, creating a relationship based on mutual trust and respect.

101

An opportunity for personal growth

Be natural. The best way to influence the situation is by simply being yourself. Being anxious to create an impression will inhibit you. Whereas if you are relaxed and spontaneous you will create just the right impression. You do not need to manipulate events. Indeed, it is best not to think too much about yourself at all. People who are on your own wavelength will be receptive to you just as you are. Always be ready to learn. Put aside your own prejudices and approach people with an open mind. Those you are meant to be involved with will respond to you favourably. Listen to the promptings of your heart. If you have allowed yourself to be deeply touched by someone or something, others will in turn be moved by you. Your sincerity will speak to something in their own hearts.

Further aspects of the situation

SIX AT THE BEGINNING
There is a faint hint of new possibilities in the air. Do not place too much importance on this as yet. Avoid weaving fantasies about something which may never happen.

SIX IN THE SECOND PLACE
Do nothing until you know more about the situation. Wait and see how events develop. If you act prematurely, you put yourself at risk of being hurt.

NINE IN THE THIRD PLACE
You are too impulsive. Do not try to force either yourself or your ideas on to others. Equally, do not allow yourself to be swept along in the wake of somebody else's enthusiasm. Use your own judgment. Exercise self-control and calm down.

NINE IN THE FOURTH PLACE
Do not try to manipulate people. Even if you succeed in influencing others in this way, you will have to be constantly striving to maintain your control. Be sincere and natural. Those you are meant to influence will respond.

NINE IN THE FIFTH PLACE
Only if you are deeply convinced of something within yourself will you be able to influence others. Otherwise, nothing significant can be achieved.

SIX AT THE TOP
You cannot influence people by talk alone. If your words are to have power, they must be backed up by something solid. Otherwise whatever you say will make little impression.

32

Perseverance

―― ――
―――――
―――――
―――――
―― ――

'Even the woodpecker owes his success to the fact that he uses his
head and keeps pecking away until he finishes the job he starts.'

Coleman Cox

The principle of perseverance, or continuity, is found everywhere in the
natural world. A tree, for instance, changes constantly as it grows from
a sapling to its full height. Yet it always remains unmistakably a tree.
This indicates that the way to approach the current situation is to be
consistent in the face of change. Do not take radical action. If something
is working for you, stay with it. Do not be blown this way and that.
Choose your path and follow it without deviating. Move slowly towards
your longer-term objective. If you have to decide between a traditional
or an innovative approach, use the tried and tested method. Keep to a
routine. If you feel the situation is stagnating, you may need to make
minor changes. But keep your goal firmly in mind. Do nothing which
might damage your chances of success. When there is a choice to be
made, always act with integrity to yourself. If things are going well, do
not allow yourself to become lazy. Even the most stable situation needs

ongoing care and attention. If matters are going badly, be patient. Do not give up.

An opportunity for personal growth

In the ancient text, this hexagram represents marriage. If your question concerns a relationship then the meaning is that you must make a commitment. But this could apply equally to a project, a job or any area currently of concern to you. If you have started something, you must see it through to the end. Practise tolerance and persistence so as to stick with things when the going gets rough. When difficulties arise, see them as a challenge to your determination and staying-power. From this point of view, a problem can give you the opportunity to strengthen yourself and your relationships. Be prepared to be flexible. There is always another person's point of view to be considered. At the same time, you must be true to yourself. Support what you sincerely believe to be right.

Further aspects of the situation

SIX AT THE BEGINNING
You want too much too soon. It is as though you are trying to run before you have learned to walk. Do not rush headlong into a new situation. Stop and consider the consequences. If you want long-term stability you must persevere. Trying to cut corners in order to get a quick result will not prove successful.

NINE IN THE SECOND PLACE
Keep a sense of balance. If you do too little, you will be ineffective in the situation. But if you try too hard, you will overstep the mark. Use your discrimination to judge how far you can safely go. Then you will have no cause for regret.

NINE IN THE THIRD PLACE
Stability must come from within, regardless of circumstances. If your state of mind depends on whatever is happening at the moment, you will never

be happy. There is no future in constantly changing your goalposts. What's more, if you are unpredictable and easily led, people will lose respect for you. And you will eventually lose respect for yourself.

NINE IN THE FOURTH PLACE
Be practical. If you are failing to achieve your goal then either it was unrealistic in the first place, or else you are setting about it in the wrong way. You have considerable determination. Use it in an area where you can actually accomplish something.

SIX IN THE FIFTH PLACE
Sometimes it is appropriate to learn from others and follow their lead. In other situations, success depends on acting independently and relying solely on your own judgment. Be flexible. Take whichever approach will be the most effective in the current circumstances.

SIX AT THE TOP
You cannot achieve your goals if you are in a state of constant agitation. Anxiety and restlessness will prevent you from forming a realistic view of your position. Calm down.

33

Retreating

'Let us make honourable retreat'
Shakespeare, *As You Like It*

Conditions are not in your favour at this time. You are recommended to
make a strategic withdrawal while you are still in a strong position. This
form of retreat is not to be confused with giving up or running away.
On the contrary, it is a powerful and constructive course of action. We
tend to think of success as consisting entirely of measurable achievement.
But there are times when you need to retreat in order to plan your next
move. It gives you an opportunity to take an overview of the situation
and reassess your priorities. There is no point in wasting valuable time
and energy struggling with an impossible situation. Distance yourself from
negative or hostile people you may be involved with. Choose your moment
carefully. Timing is essential. Avoid a head-on confrontation. You cannot
win and would only weaken your resources.

An opportunity for personal growth

The challenge is to make a retreat without losing your dignity. If you are under attack, or feel that you have been misrepresented, your pride may have taken a knock. As a result, you could be tempted to try and get your own point of view across at all costs. But this will only make matters worse. You would become more deeply entangled in a battle you cannot win. There is too much going against you at this point. Control your emotions. Stay calm and retreat within yourself. If you withdraw your involvement and are unavailable for argument, you cannot be injured.

Drawing this hexagram can also indicate the need to retreat from a particular lifestyle which does not serve your best interests. If there are no moving lines and therefore no further hexagram, it may indicate that it would be best to leave the situation permanently. Alternatively, you could benefit from a literal period of retreat and should consider having some time away in order to recharge your batteries.

Further aspects of the situation

SIX AT THE BEGINNING
Stay calm and do nothing. It would have been better to withdraw your involvement earlier. Attempting to act now would be disastrous. You must be patient and wait.

SIX IN THE SECOND PLACE
If you are absolutely determined to do the right thing, you will succeed. It could help your cause to cooperate with someone who is in a position to advise you.

NINE IN THE THIRD PLACE
You are prevented from leaving a situation which is not in your own best interests. It may be that your own fears and anxieties are stopping you. Do not try to hide behind someone else or expect them to fight your battles for you. Stand up for yourself. Try to stay centred and detached, particularly if those around you have a negative outlook. If you allow yourself to be drawn in, you risk feeling drained.

NINE IN THE FOURTH PLACE
Make your retreat with courtesy and grace. Do not be influenced by what others may say or do to try and stop you. Stay as uninvolved as you possibly can. This will help you to avoid being drawn into a game of one-upmanship which would harm your position. If you refuse to be involved, the only ones to suffer will be those you leave behind.

NINE IN THE FIFTH PLACE
If you choose the right moment, you will be able to retreat from the situation in a perfectly friendly fashion. Stand firmly but politely by your decision and do not be put off by irrelevant considerations.

NINE AT THE TOP
You are absolutely clear in your own mind that you must now withdraw from the situation. Because you have no doubts about your course of action, you can quite happily go your own way. Doing so will bring you great success.

34

Great Power

'Be not afraid of greatness: some men are born great, some achieve greatness and some have greatness thrust upon them'.

Shakespeare, *Twelfth Night*

You can have a dynamic effect on the situation. But the fact that you are in a strong position gives you a responsibility to use it well. Do not be aggressive or domineering. Before making a decision, carefully consider what would be of most benefit to all concerned. Be open to advice and to the views of others. If you insist on going your own way regardless, you will create opposition. At the end of the day, however, you must listen to your own conscience and do what is right. Refuse to be side-tracked by any considerations which are not central to the issue. Once you know what must be done, do not act impulsively or try to hurry things to suit yourself. Wait for the right time. Then take decisive action.

An opportunity for personal growth

Those who have real power are the ones who least need to use it. Individuals who show off and try to dominate others are not powerful. They are insecure people trying to make themselves feel powerful. Be patient, tolerant and respectful of the feelings of others. Play by the rules. Think before you act. If you rush into things like a bull in a china shop, you will create havoc. Do not be tempted to throw your weight around or manipulate others for your own ends. If you abuse your position in any way, sooner or later your actions will rebound on you. Be determined to do what is right. Keep any self-indulgent tendencies firmly under control.

Further aspects of the situation

NINE AT THE BEGINNING
However strong and confident you feel, the conditions are not favourable for you to push ahead. If you act recklessly, you will lose credibility. Be content with taking some preparatory steps. Do not invest all your energy or resources at this stage. Over-enthusiasm at the beginning of a situation usually fades quickly.

NINE IN THE SECOND PLACE
With no serious opposition to hinder you, progress can now be made. Do not let this make you careless. Everything will turn out well provided that you do not become over-confident.

NINE IN THE THIRD PLACE
The more truly powerful a person is, the less he or she needs to use that power. By openly displaying your strength, you will attract hostility. Do not try to force matters in any way.

NINE IN THE FOURTH PLACE
Provided that you use your influence in the right way, obstacles will vanish. The best way to overcome resistance is to proceed quietly and very patiently, one step at a time. Bear in mind the principle of water wearing down a stone.

111

SIX IN THE FIFTH PLACE

The situation has changed for the better. Now, nothing stands in your way. This means that there is absolutely no need to be stubborn or aggressive. You can resolve the situation harmoniously.

SIX AT THE TOP

The situation has reached stalemate. You can make no further progress. If you persist in trying to force results, you will make things even more complicated. Stop struggling. Resign yourself to the fact that there is nothing more you can do. If you are to resolve this issue, you must find a different approach.

35

Progress

```
━━━  ━ ━
━━━  ━ ━
━━━  ━ ━
```

'Ye are the light of the world. A city that is set on a hill cannot be hid.'

Matthew 5

Rapid progress is now possible. Your abilities are recognized and appreciated. You have the opportunity to shine in a position in which they will be used. Be sincere and generous. Your own personal progress depends on using your gifts unselfishly. The more you help someone else to flourish, the stronger your own position will become. A clear mind will enable you to shed light on all aspects of the situation at this time. Have faith in your insights and communicate them to others. Because you have the right ideas, you can have a good deal of influence on the situation. This will work to the benefit of everybody concerned. You, in turn, will receive ongoing support from the people you need.

An opportunity for personal growth

What matters here is not so much what you *do* as who you *are*. Within each one of us is a spark of divinity. When you are in touch with your inmost truth you are in contact with this spirit. As we go through life, this clear, direct vision becomes clouded over. We become hypnotized and conditioned by other people's opinions as to what is right. Now, in order to continue making progress, you must discover your own deepest values and live by them. If your life-style is incompatible with your true nature, you cannot be happy. Have the courage of your convictions and speak your truth. Do not worry about whether or not others approve of you. What matters most of all is to live in harmony with yourself. Your life will then unfold in exactly the right way.

Further aspects of the situation

SIX AT THE BEGINNING
Do not be discouraged if others lack confidence in your abilities. Have faith in yourself. Although you may be unable to make progress at present, you will eventually succeed.

SIX IN THE SECOND PLACE
Progress is blocked. You are unable to make contact with somebody who could help you. Do not be depressed. The setback is temporary. If you persevere, the breakthrough will come. You will find the assistance you need. A woman may be helpful to you in this respect.

SIX IN THE THIRD PLACE
Although you may prefer to be totally independent, further progress depends on support from others. Do not be too proud to accept their contribution. You will find it both helpful and encouraging.

NINE IN THE FOURTH PLACE
You are offered an opportunity to make progress. Taking it would involve you in questionable activities or methods. Inevitably you would be found

out. You would appear in a very bad light. Is it worth compromising yourself?

SIX IN THE FIFTH PLACE
You may be concerned because you have failed to take maximum advantage of an opportunity. Do not worry. You are in a very fortunate position. Whether or not you have left certain things undone is irrelevant. It will not affect the final outcome. The most important thing is to continue to make progress. This will ensure that everything works out successfully.

NINE AT THE TOP
Misfortune will be the result of trying to force any further developments. The situation will get out of hand. Exercise self-control. Accept that you have gone as far as you can. Avoid being aggressive towards others.

36

Keeping a Low Profile

――　――
――　――
――――

'A soft answer turneth away wrath: but grievous words stir
up anger.'

Proverbs 15

Your environment is hostile to you in some respect. But circumstances are
such that there is no way out. In due course this will change. In the meantime,
you have no choice but to resign yourself to keeping a very low profile. If you
try to communicate your views, you will meet with a negative response. Your
values are quite different to those of the people around you. Protect yourself
by allowing them to think you accept the position. You could well be the
object of somebody's envy or resentment. Act in your own best interests. Do
not provoke arguments or act aggressively. You must not lose sight of your
own goals, but your determination to achieve them has to remain hidden for
the time being. Refuse to let anything others may say or do undermine your
stability and self-confidence. Keep your own beliefs well and truly alive in
the depths of your heart. In due course, you will emerge the winner.

An opportunity for personal growth

Your challenge is to keep yourself to yourself and avoid confrontation. Hide your light under a bushel. To let it shine would be harmful. Others are not sympathetic to you. However strongly you feel, you must let things pass and bide your time. This can be particularly difficult if others cannot see what is perfectly obvious to you. Do not be tempted to point out the error of their ways. This would only make matters worse. All you can do is remain true to yourself and take a back seat. Keep your thoughts and feelings to yourself and try to appear courteous and amenable. Look after yourself and wait for the situation to improve. Meditation or prayer would help you at this time.

Further aspects of the situation

NINE AT THE BEGINNING

You cannot rise above the current difficulties. In order to protect your own interests and avoid compromising yourself, you need to withdraw from the situation and move on.

SIX IN THE SECOND PLACE

You have run into serious difficulties. A lesser person might be devastated by this turn of events. But you must take up the challenge. Let it spur you on to take action which will help everybody involved. Stay calm and keep your wits about you. By clever use of your resources, you can salvage the situation.

NINE IN THE THIRD PLACE

In the process of pursuing your aim, the source of the problem has become clear to you. You must be uncompromising in your determination to tackle it. Difficulties have arisen as a result of negative attitudes, whether your own or another's. Either way, you must proceed slowly and carefully. The situation has taken a long time to develop. Change for the better will therefore not happen overnight.

117

SIX IN THE FOURTH PLACE
Your clear understanding has left you with no illusions. There is no possibility that matters will improve. The best course of action is therefore to remove yourself from the situation altogether.

SIX IN THE FIFTH PLACE
Your ability to persevere in the face of difficulties is being put to the test. You are having to endure a most uncomfortable position. To some extent you are a victim of circumstances over which you have no control. There is therefore no point in putting up a fight. Nevertheless you must not give up. Hide your true thoughts and feelings for the time being. Be extremely cautious. Eventually your patience and self-control will be rewarded.

SIX AT THE TOP
The situation has become as bad as it can be. Power which could have been put to positive and creative use has been misused for harmful purposes. This state of affairs will inevitably disintegrate, allowing something far better to develop. It is a law of nature that when darkness has run its course, the light always returns.

37

The Family

```
━━━  ━━━
━━━  ━━━
━━━━━━━━
━━━  ━━━
━━━━━━━━
━━━━━━━━
```

'I do hate to be unquiet at home.'
Samuel Pepys

Family concerns are highlighted here. This does not necessarily mean the traditional set-up of father, mother and children. Any two or more people who share their lives on a day-to-day basis by living or working together would constitute a 'family' in this instance. What matters is to keep your house in order. This could literally mean that some clearing-out or home maintenance is required. Or it may be that family relationships need attention. Mutual affection and support are the necessary ingredients for a happy communal life. Relationships which work well do so because those concerned show respect for each other. But all too often, alas, it is a case of familiarity breeding contempt. Living at close quarters can result in people behaving with a lack of courtesy which would be unthinkable in the outside world. Consideration for those closest to you is what will carry relationships safely through difficult times.

119

An opportunity for personal growth

Be cooperative and willing to fulfil your particular function within the family or closely-knit group in question. Do not insist on asserting yourself. Be receptive to the needs of others so that you can contribute to their well-being. Avoid asking people to do what you would not be prepared to do yourself. If you are to be taken seriously, your words must have power. Say what you mean and mean what you say. If you practise what you preach, you will gain authority and win respect. Do your best to be gentle and tolerant. But do not hesitate to be firm and exert your authority when necessary. It would be wrong, for instance, to tolerate destructive or anti-social behaviour within the family unit.

Further aspects of the situation

NINE AT THE BEGINNING

Right at the beginning of any endeavour, the role and responsibilities of each person involved must be clearly defined. Make sure that everybody knows exactly where they stand. This helps to minimize the risk of matters getting out of hand in future. Once a bad habit or a negative pattern of behaviour is allowed to take hold, it becomes much harder to deal with.

SIX IN THE SECOND PLACE

Quietly pay attention to your immediate responsibilities. Carry them out to the best of your ability. Don't try and take on anything more. Avoid acting on impulse.

NINE IN THE THIRD PLACE

Words spoken in anger can cause endless damage. Bad temper must be controlled and respect for others encouraged. Within any group there must be discipline. But it must not be too strict. On balance, however, it is better to err on the side of severity than to be over-indulgent. If you are too permissive, the result will be chaos.

SIX IN THE FOURTH PLACE
Be willing to be of service to others. Your support is immensely valuable to all concerned and will bring great rewards.

NINE IN THE FIFTH PLACE
An atmosphere of mutual trust and affection is indicated. This is the basis of happiness in relationships. If you have a position of authority, use it to care for those who depend on you rather than to exercise control over them.

NINE AT THE TOP
The best way to influence others is to be true to yourself. Do not try to exert authority. If you faithfully carry out your responsibilities, people will respect and trust you.

38

Opposition

'Without contraries is no progression. Attraction and Repulsion, Reason and Energy, Love and Hate, are necessary to Human existence.'

William Blake

Disagreements are indicated here. Misunderstandings have led to conflict between those involved. Doubt and mistrust prevent cooperation. Under these circumstances, no serious progress can be made. Avoid unnecessary confrontation. Be willing to meet others half-way. A creative move of this kind can change the atmosphere. Hard attitudes soften just a little. The door to reconciliation opens, if only a fraction. Tread carefully because you can do only a limited amount at this time. Above all, be tolerant. This will create the possibility of finding common ground on which to build. Do not confuse tolerance with weakness. Only a strong person has the self-respect and generosity of heart it takes to be tolerant.

An opportunity for personal growth

There are times when opposition can be extremely useful. If you can work out your differences with others, new life is brought into the situation. But you must preserve your dignity. It is not a matter of giving in. You must certainly support your own point of view. At the same time you need to be willing to listen to the other side. Remember that opposites are essential to the life process. Their meeting can create stimulus and excitement. Alternatively, of course, they can fight and make life miserable for each other. It all depends on your attitude. If you can genuinely respect and learn from each other's point of view, the period of opposition will be beneficial to all concerned.

Further aspects of the situation

NINE AT THE BEGINNING
Where there is a misunderstanding, do not try and force a reconciliation. Allow things to work themselves out at their own pace. The set-back is only temporary. You cannot lose what truly belongs in your life. If you are dealing with hostile people, keep them at a polite distance. Reacting aggressively will involve you unnecessarily in further conflict.

NINE IN THE SECOND PLACE
Be open to an unexpected or unusual turn of events. It will benefit you in some way. You may meet somebody you instantly recognize as a kindred spirit. Destiny is at work here.

SIX IN THE THIRD PLACE
One problem seems to follow another. Whatever you try to do is blocked. Do not give up. Support what you know to be right. In the end the situation will turn out well.

NINE IN THE FOURTH PLACE
Feelings of isolation will not last. You will meet somebody of like mind who you can trust and who will cooperate with you.

SIX IN THE FIFTH PLACE

Somebody is genuine in their desire for a reconciliation. Yet you have misgivings. But the person involved has your best interests at heart and can help you. Accept the olive branch and be willing to cooperate.

NINE AT THE TOP

Misunderstandings have led you to question the motives of people who in fact mean you well. It would be to your advantage to drop your defences and meet those concerned half-way. If you can stop seeing wrongs where there are none, relationships will take on a new lease of life.

39

Facing Obstruction

‎☰ ☵

'We shall not fail or falter; we shall not weaken or tire.'
Sir Winston Churchill

In the face of apparently insurmountable problems, you feel stuck. There seems to be no way forward. Whatever you do fails to have any real effect. In fact the more you struggle to resolve the issue, the worse matters become. The answer is to stop trying to make things work. Accept that you simply don't know what to do. What *is* clear is that your current strategy is not effective. You need to explore other avenues of approach. But, as things stand, you can no longer see the wood for the trees. How are you to arrive at a more detached point of view? The answer is to let go of your involvement in the situation for the time being. This does not mean simply giving up. On the contrary, you must be absolutely determined to achieve your aim. But the first step towards success is to disengage yourself from a position which is obviously leading nowhere.

An opportunity for personal growth

It is unproductive to blame other people, or circumstances, for the current problems. The real obstacle to progress lies within yourself. A change of attitude is called for. Then you will be able to move forward. Looked at in this way, an apparently frustrating situation can become a useful source of information. It indicates that you have something to learn. Do you, for instance, expect too much of other people? Or perhaps you make unrealistic demands of yourself or are too impatient for results. In one way or another, this is a golden opportunity for self-development. To make the most of it, don't be too proud to ask for advice and support. Approach people who understand what you are hoping to achieve. Their input, coming from a different perspective, will inspire you and help revive your spirits.

Further aspects of the situation

SIX AT THE BEGINNING
Hold back and do nothing for the moment. Trying to force the issue would be counterproductive. The opportunity to take further action will come in due course.

SIX IN THE SECOND PLACE
Like it or not, you have to tackle the problem head on. There is no choice. Any misgivings must take second place to your wider responsibilities.

NINE IN THE THIRD PLACE
It is not safe to take direct action, however tempted you are to do so. You would put at risk both your own security and that of others.

SIX IN THE FOURTH PLACE
You do not have the necessary resources to deal with the situation by yourself. Accept help from people you know are dependable and trustworthy.

NINE IN THE FIFTH PLACE

In spite of serious obstacles, you must refuse to be deflected from your goal. Be absolutely determined to face the difficulties and resolve them. You will attract help from people who are impressed by your strength of character. They will therefore be willing to cooperate with you. The results will be beneficial to all concerned.

SIX AT THE TOP

You may be tempted to bury your head in the sand and pretend that the problems are not your concern. But the truth is that you have a responsibility to be involved. In order to resolve the situation, a cooperative effort is needed, and your particular input is essential to a successful outcome.

40

Release from Obstruction

```
___   ___
___   ___
_____
___   ___
_____
___   ___
```

'I was angry with my friend; I told my wrath, my wrath did end.'
William Blake

You have come to the end of a frustrating cycle during which your
progress has been blocked. In matters of relationship issues there have
been misunderstandings and conflict. Now your difficulties can at last
be resolved. Projects can come to fruition. You can move away from a
situation which does not fulfil you. But none of this will happen without
your active cooperation. Your role is to understand the factors which have
been holding you back. Consider where you have been blocked and why.
Look at how your own actions or behaviour may have contributed. Be
prepared to act on your insights and make some changes where you can.
Many of the obstacles will then fade away quite naturally. This will bring
relief from accumulated stress and anxiety. You can then return to a regular
and much more satisfying routine. But do not procrastinate. Now is the time
to take the bull by the horns.

An opportunity for personal growth

You must deal with unresolved emotional issues. Holding on to hostility, regret or old grievances keeps you locked into the past. Letting them go clears the air and frees you to live more fully in the present. Do not dwell on another's faults or mistakes. Blame and criticism will not improve matters or bring you peace of mind. You cannot change others. But if you are prepared to be generous, you can change yourself and acquire a more positive outlook. In the process, you will cease to feel like a victim of circumstances. If you feel hurt or annoyed, do not brood or nurture resentment. Bring matters out into the open. Try to show some goodwill. Be willing to reconcile misunderstandings. Put the past behind you, where it belongs. Then you can go forward to meet the future with renewed energy and confidence.

Further aspects of the situation

SIX AT THE BEGINNING
You have done what you can. Now you can simply relax, rest and recuperate your energy. Action would be premature.

NINE IN THE SECOND PLACE
A destructive element is at work in the situation. It could take the form of ill will from others or negative attitudes within yourself. Either way, the effect is to undermine your position. Unless you take action to stop this you could lose a valuable opportunity. Provided you are totally honest and straightforward, you will succeed.

SIX IN THE THIRD PLACE
You have come some way towards achieving a difficult goal. But there is still much hard work to be done. Be aware of your limitations. If you persist in doing something for which you are not really suited, or which is beyond your current capabilities, you risk being humiliated.

NINE IN THE FOURTH PLACE
Certain people have involved themselves with you for selfish reasons of their own. They do not have your best interests at heart. You must detach yourself from these unhealthy relationships. They are preventing you from developing sincere friendships with people who would otherwise be willing to cooperate with you.

SIX IN THE FIFTH PLACE
To make the most of life, you must be determined to free yourself from involvement with whoever or whatever drags you down. Develop a positive attitude to yourself. Be committed to your own well-being. Become your own best friend. Then you will no longer attract harmful people or circumstances.

SIX AT THE TOP
The last and most powerful obstacle to progress can now be overcome. Make careful plans for dealing with it. Wait until the time is ripe and then take appropriate action. If your timing is accurate you will hit the mark perfectly. Nothing will then stand between you and success.

41

Decrease

```
━━━━━  ━━━━━
━━━━━  ━━━━━
━━━━━  ━━━━━
━━━━━━━━━━━
```

'"That's the reason they're called lessons," the Gryphon remarked:
"because they lessen from day to day."'
Lewis Carroll, *Alice in Wonderland*

DECREASE implies having less of something. This is part of a natural
cycle of events and is therefore unavoidable. It means accepting that you
must give up something or some aspect of your life. This will be to your
advantage in the longer term. Take stock of the situation and decide
where your priorities lie. Simplify your life accordingly. You may feel at
a disadvantage compared to others who have more than you do. But in
this situation who you are is far more important than what you have in
the material sense. What matters above all is to be sincere. Do not pretend
to be something you are not. Have faith in yourself and act with integrity.
You will find that others respond positively. Be prepared to give rather than
expecting to be given to. If you have to take a back seat, do so gracefully.
Do not worry about the outcome. Great success is indicated.

An opportunity for personal growth.

Do not over-react. In respect of your personality, DECREASE involves overcoming self-indulgence. It means being in control of your emotions rather than letting them run away with you. Making a drama out of the situation will prevent you from having a balanced perspective. Do not confuse molehills with mountains. Exercise self-restraint. Be open to different ways of doing things. Do not insist on trying to get your own way. Be prepared to make a positive contribution to the situation. Putting your abilities at the service of others will help you to develop your own potential. This will inevitably bring good fortune.

Further aspects of the situation

NINE IN THE FIRST PLACE
Complete the tasks for which you are responsible. You can then offer your assistance to others. Give only as much as is needed to help them to help themselves. Think about what you are doing. It is not useful to give somebody so much help that they become dependent on you. This also holds true in reverse. Do not take from another more than is absolutely necessary.

NINE IN THE SECOND PLACE
Give only as much as feels comfortable for you. Do nothing which goes against the grain. Keep your dignity and self-respect intact. Only from this standpoint are you in a position to truly help others. You serve nobody, least of all yourself, by catering to the unreasonable expectations of others.

SIX IN THE THIRD PLACE
Two's company and three's a crowd and makes for an unbalanced situation. If you stand alone, you will get the help you need. Whereas if you try to become part of an established partnership because you fear being alone, problems are bound to arise. Do not try to force matters. Wait until the solution presents itself.

SIX IN THE FOURTH PLACE

A negative outlook is bad for your well-being and can only isolate you. If you project ill will, people who could help you will not feel inspired to seek out your company. Instead of being critical of others, focus on dealing with your own shortcomings. By developing a more positive outlook, you will attract friends and helpers. Life will be far more enjoyable.

SIX IN THE FIFTH PLACE

You have nothing to worry about. Fate is on your side. Working to improve yourself now brings great rewards. Nothing can prevent your success and good fortune.

NINE AT THE TOP

You have a great deal to contribute. Be unselfish. Look at the wider picture. Offer your resources in the service of others. People will be willing to help you achieve your aims. The more you give, the more you and everybody else will benefit.

42

Increase

```
━━━━━━━
━━━━━━━
━━━  ━━━
━━━  ━━━
━━━  ━━━
━━━━━━━
```

'There is a tide in the affairs of men
Which, taken at the flood, leads on to fortune;'
Shakespeare, *Julius Caesar*

The tide of fortune is flowing in your favour. Problems can now be resolved. Relationships and projects flourish. New opportunities beckon. Considerable change is possible. Even difficult tasks can be tackled successfully. But it is up to you to make the most of this favourable period. It will not last indefinitely. Now is the time to take whatever action is needed to move matters forward. If you have been dithering, make a decision. Have the courage to make a leap in the dark if necessary. The outcome will be successful. INCREASE implies reaching out and being of benefit to others. Anything you attempt purely out of self-interest will not attract success. Whereas what you offer freely and generously will return to you in many ways. Think in terms of what you can contribute to the situation rather than what you can get out of it.

An opportunity for personal growth

INCREASE indicates that many possibilities are open to you. Aim high now and give of your very best. A positive outlook will help you to play to your strengths. Negative attitudes – especially about yourself – are like excess baggage. They weigh you down unnecessarily and interfere with your freedom of movement. To release them takes self-discipline and a commitment to your own best interests. This is hard work but brings huge rewards in terms of your overall well-being. It may be helpful to adopt as a role model someone whose good qualities you admire. Practise demonstrating these qualities in your own life.

Further aspects of the situation

NINE AT THE BEGINNING
Fortune is on your side. Worthwhile aims can now be accomplished. This is the time to tackle something which perhaps you would normally dismiss as being beyond your capabilities. Provided that you act from unselfish motives, the outcome will be highly successful.

SIX IN THE SECOND PLACE
Fate smiles upon you so that your affairs flourish. Your own generosity of spirit will ensure that you continue to attract good fortune. Keep your feet on the ground. Attend to the details of everyday life as usual.

SIX IN THE THIRD PLACE
Although the situation is difficult, conditions are such that it will turn out to your advantage. Be extremely conscientious about doing the right thing. Your integrity will be appreciated. Such difficult times can in fact be very useful. In learning how to cope with them, you acquire invaluable experience and skills.

SIX IN THE FOURTH PLACE
Be open to new and different points of view. If you find yourself acting as a mediator, do not take sides. Your responsibility is to ensure that everybody

involved somehow benefits from the situation. In doing so, you will win the trust and respect of all concerned.

NINE IN THE FIFTH PLACE
If you have that rarest of qualities, a truly kind heart, you have no need to ask about the results of your actions. Your genuine concern for others ensures that everything you do will turn out for the best. Other people cannot fail to recognize your worth.

NINE AT THE TOP
Although you have the ability to benefit others, you are failing to do so. This attitude will attract hostility, bringing you nothing but misfortune. You must stop taking and start giving.

43

Determination

_____ ___
_____
_____
_____
_____
_____ ___

'"Begin at the beginning," the King said gravely, "and go on till you come to the end: then stop."'

Lewis Carroll, *Alice's Adventures in Wonderland*

You must take a firm stand. An obstacle of some kind has to be overcome. It will not disappear of its own accord. Matters have reached a point where allowing them to drift on would involve you in an unacceptable compromise. You must be quite clear in your own mind that the situation has to change and be determined to do something about it. But it is essential to proceed with caution. Make sure you know what you are up against. Do not over-react or go on the offensive. It will not serve your purposes to trigger a hostile attitude in others. Be courteous but firm. Although you must make your views plain, try to do so in a way which causes minimum offence. Keep a balanced perspective. If the issue is one of difficulties in a close relationship, nothing will be gained by either party blaming the other. Make sure that grievances are given a thorough airing. Then be determined to put the past behind you.

An opportunity for personal growth

If you are objecting to somebody else's behaviour, check first that it is not a case of the pot calling the kettle black. Otherwise you will simply be giving whoever is involved ammunition to use against you. If you are quite certain that the problem lies outside yourself, go ahead and tackle it. If not, then look first at the role you yourself have played in the matter. Make a resolution not to gloss over your own shortcomings. Use them as a basis for further self-development. But do not become obsessed with your weak spots. It is much better for your confidence to focus instead on developing your strengths. This will enable you to make a positive contribution to the situation. If you have an open mind, you will find much to learn.

Further aspects of the situation

NINE AT THE BEGINNING
However determined you may be, you are not strong enough to tackle the problem head-on. Be cautious. Keep well within your limits. If you over-estimate your capabilities, you could seriously jeopardize your position.

NINE IN THE SECOND PLACE
Be on the alert for signs of trouble. Difficulties could arise at any time. If you are prepared to meet them, your position will be safe.

NINE IN THE THIRD PLACE
It is up to you to cope with a disruptive force in the way you think best. Others may misunderstand your approach. But as long as you know the reasons for what you are doing, you will emerge unscathed.

NINE IN THE FOURTH PLACE
It will not serve your best interests to insist on doing things in your own way. If you would only be less stubborn and more willing to listen to good advice, the situation could be satisfactorily resolved.

138

NINE IN THE FIFTH PLACE

Be determined not to give up the struggle against persistent difficulties. You need to get down to the roots of the problem and deal with those. However you decide to go about this, be sure to act with integrity.

SIX AT THE TOP

On the surface, it looks as though the problems are resolved. You may now be tempted to relax your guard. But do not delude yourself. There are still lurking difficulties. You cannot afford to be lulled into a false sense of security.

44

A Meeting of Opposites

'Beware, as long as you live, of judging people by appearances.'
Jean de la Fontaine

If you feel uneasy about the situation, even though you don't quite know why, you must trust your instincts. It may well be that somebody does not have your best interests at heart. If someone has made you an offer, be careful. Pay great attention to what they have to say. Notice whether their words match up with their behaviour. There is a real danger that you could compromise your personal dignity and integrity. The way to avoid this is to be determined not to allow anybody else to have power over you. Don't be afraid to make your own views clear. If people realize that you cannot be taken in, they are unlikely to waste their time trying to convince you. Not all offers, of course, are suspect. In a situation where you are sure of the other person's good intent, being prepared to meet them half-way will be great benefit to you both.

An opportunity for personal growth

Hidden dangers lurk in an apparently agreeable situation. If you indulge in a seemingly harmless temptation, it may well develop in an unforeseen way and cause you trouble. Be cautious. Stick firmly to the path you know is right for you. If you are aware that a bad habit is creeping into your life, do not allow it to develop further. Any problem is best dealt with in its early stages. If it is allowed to get a hold on the situation, it can all too quickly get out of hand. This applies equally to negative ways of thinking. Unless you control such thoughts as soon as they arise, they can begin to colour your entire outlook.

Further aspects of the situation

SIX AT THE BEGINNING
Something very destructive is beginning to make its presence felt. You must take action to stop this before it can develop further and do any harm. Do not allow yourself to be possessed by negative thoughts or emotions.

NINE IN THE SECOND PLACE
Be determined to resist negative ways of thinking. Keep them under control, both for your own sake and that of others who could be affected. Equally, do not allow yourself to be influenced by the pessimistic attitudes of people around you.

NINE IN THE THIRD PLACE
You are faced with temptation. A seductive opportunity beckons and you would like to be involved. Fortunately, circumstances are such that this is not possible. Yet you are left in a state of indecision. Consider the issue very carefully. A deeper understanding will ensure that you do not make a serious mistake.

NINE IN THE FOURTH PLACE
Do not be stand-offish towards certain people because you think they are unimportant. You do not know when you might need their help. Be courteous and tolerant. You will then be able to rely on their support in the future.

NINE IN THE FIFTH PLACE
Carry on quietly doing your best. Do not try to impress others or convince them of your point of view. If you do the right thing in the right way, you will automatically succeed in achieving your aim. You have nothing to gain by trying to manipulate the situation.

NINE AT THE TOP
You may want to distance yourself from certain people whose company you find irksome. It might be less traumatic to simply withdraw quietly than to make some kind of statement of your intentions. Either way, you will not be popular. But because you are doing what you have to, you will not be unduly concerned about other people's reactions.

45

Gathering Together

```
___  ___
_____
_____
___   ___
___  ___
___   ___
```

'Come then, let us go forward together with our united strength.'
Sir Winston Churchill

When people gather together in large groups such as families or organizations, there are times when conflict is inevitable. Yet it is to everybody's advantage for the group to work harmoniously. If people are pulling in different directions, the community will fall apart. Whatever your position in the group, be prepared to play your part unselfishly. As a member of the community, give your support to the leader. If you have a position of responsibility or leadership, give the best of which you are capable to the group. No matter what the circumstances may be, stand up for what you know to be true. Keep on your toes. If you can anticipate potential difficulties, you can take appropriate steps to nip them in the bud. Try to act in the best interests of all concerned.

An opportunity for personal growth

You must keep yourself together. This is especially true if you are in a position of leadership. If you are in conflict with yourself, you will accomplish nothing. Keep your goal firmly in mind. If there are difficulties in your environment, do not be thrown off balance. Let nothing shake your faith in yourself and what you are doing. Whatever the challenges you face, you must remain calm. Live up to the best in yourself and do what you know to be right and true. If people know they can depend on you, they will give you their confidence and respect.

Further aspects of the situation

SIX AT THE BEGINNING
You may be confused and therefore hesitant about committing yourself. Do not be discouraged if things are not going according to plan. Help is at hand. You have only to ask for it.

SIX IN THE SECOND PLACE
If you feel attracted to a particular group or organization, trust your instincts. You would be right to join. Because a natural empathy exists between you and those involved, you will be accepted without difficulty. It is a case of discovering kindred spirits.

SIX IN THE THIRD PLACE
The group you would like to join is a closed circle. Do not try to push your way in. Swallow your pride and take a more humble approach. Make an ally of somebody whose position within the group is already well established. Let them introduce you.

NINE IN THE FOURTH PLACE
Your motives are impeccable. You have sacrificed self-interest in order to work for the greater good of the whole. This will bring you great success.

NINE IN THE FIFTH PLACE
A person who has the role of leader cannot depend on their position alone to win respect. He or she has to earn the trust of others by virtue of their personal qualities. They must demonstrate a whole-hearted commitment to the well-being of the group.

SIX AT THE TOP
Your efforts to make a contribution are not appreciated. But this is not your fault. Your motives have been misunderstood. Do not try to hide the fact that you feel hurt. This may cause the person or people concerned to revise their opinions.

46

Pushing Upward

```
___   ___
___   ___
_____
___   ___
```

'There must be a beginning of any great matter, but the continuing
unto the end until it be thoroughly finished yields the true glory.'
Sir Francis Drake

This is a most favourable time for you. Indeed, it is at times like this that
dreams can come true. Aim high, for nothing can stop you. Conditions are
such that every move you make will lead you closer to certain success. You
will meet with great good fortune. Nothing can stop it. You have no reason
at all to be anxious. The foundations of your success are already firmly in
place. All you need do is keep your head. Carry on making steady progress,
one step at a time. Believe in yourself and your abilities. You have every
reason to be positive and optimistic. If anything appears to be standing
in your way, it can now be easily dealt with. Relationships will thrive now.
Do not hesitate to approach people who have the necessary authority or
influence to help you. You can be confident of getting all the support you
need. Your efforts will gain recognition. It is time for you to step into the
spotlight.

An opportunity for personal growth

Make a commitment to bringing out the best in yourself. Do not be willing to settle for anything less. Decide what it is that you value most. Consider the direction in which you want your life to go. Once you know where your priorities lie, make sure that you put them into practice in your everyday life. Let them be the basis for the decisions you make daily, no matter how large or small. Each choice you make in your ordinary, day-to-day life can lead you one step nearer to your goal. It is a matter of acquiring self-discipline. Great achievements are the result of ongoing, unwavering progress.

Further aspects of the situation

SIX AT THE BEGINNING
Your determination to succeed is recognized by people who have the influence to further your cause. Their confidence in your abilities will help you to achieve your goal.

NINE IN THE SECOND PLACE
You are not, on the face of it, in a strong position. Your resources are limited. But if you genuinely want to make a contribution, you will meet with a favourable response. Others will be impressed by your sincerity.

NINE IN THE THIRD PLACE
Your progress is effortless. Nothing at all stands in your way. It is all so easy that you might well feel apprehensive. But you have no need to worry provided that you continue to act in good faith. Carry on in the way you are going.

SIX IN THE FOURTH PLACE
The situation is extremely favourable. You are now in a position to attain your goals.

SIX IN THE FIFTH PLACE

As a result of steady progress, you are well on the way to achieving your goal. Do not be tempted to take short cuts. Ultimate success will be the result of making progress step by step. Pay attention to detail.

SIX AT THE TOP

Be discriminating. Do not take any further steps without the most careful consideration. Avoid acting on impulse. Do you need to carry things further at this time? Are you deluding yourself? Assess the situation carefully. Otherwise you risk losing all you have gained.

47

Being Restricted

——— ———
—————————
——— ———
—————————
——— ———

'Where griping griefs the heart would wound,
And doleful dumps the mind oppress . . .'
Anon., *A Song to the Lute in Musicke*

You are trapped in an oppressive situation which is beyond your control. Life appears to be conspiring against you. There is nothing you can do at this point to change things for the better. The situation will improve in due course. In the meantime, do not waste your energy or resources trying to struggle against the odds. Hold back and wait. There is no point in trying to influence others at present. Your words will only fall on deaf ears. All in all, you may well feel at the end of your tether. Yet there is one thing you can do. That is to hold tightly on to your faith in yourself. Nothing can destroy this unless you allow it to. You must remain absolutely determined to succeed. With inner strength, you can survive this period and come out winning.

An opportunity for personal growth

You must summon up all your resources of determination and will-power. Do not allow yourself to be dragged down by circumstances or wallow in self-pity. Life is not always fair. Yet the show must go on. If you give in to depression, you will be the ultimate loser. You owe it to yourself to think positively. Fight your negative thoughts and feelings tooth and nail. Anybody can be optimistic when things are going well. It takes considerably more effort to stay positive in difficult times like these. But if you succeed, you will gain immensely in terms of your inner strength and self-confidence.

Further aspects of the situation

SIX AT THE BEGINNING
Matters have reached a very low point indeed. You can see no light at the end of the tunnel. Giving in to your fears and doubts will make you feel even worse, creating a vicious circle of negativity. Refuse to see yourself as a victim of circumstances.

NINE IN THE SECOND PLACE
Outwardly there are no major problems. You have what you need. Yet you are bored or unaccountably depressed. Life seems banal, meaningless. Possibly you have become too self-indulgent or have made too many compromises in order to be comfortable. But help is on the way provided that you are willing to be of service to others. Getting involved in something beyond your own personal interests will give you back your zest for living.

SIX IN THE THIRD PLACE
You need to get your priorities straight. You turn first one way and then another and look for support in the wrong places. Your impatience and indecisiveness prevent you from seeing what is before your eyes. You then make mountains out of molehills. Calm down and get matters in perspective.

NINE IN THE FOURTH PLACE
Your intentions are good. Doubts have crept in, however, and made you slow to act. It is therefore all too easy for you to be side-tracked almost before you have begun. This is a source of embarrassment. But if you remain determined to achieve your aim, you will succeed.

NINE IN THE FIFTH PLACE
The position is frustrating. You have excellent intentions and the ability to carry them out, but you cannot get the help you need. People misunderstand your motives. Be patient and calm. Little by little, the situation will change for the better.

SIX AT THE TOP
The difficulties are coming to an end. You can quite easily break free from whatever has been holding you back. Put the past behind you. Nothing now stands in your way except your own attitudes. Do not allow yesterday's bad experiences to stop you from facing today with confidence or looking forward to tomorrow with optimism.

48

The Wellsprings of Life

'Man is asked to make of himself what he is supposed to become
to fulfil his destiny.'

Paul Tillich

To deal with this situation successfully you must go deeply into things. If
you judge by appearances or what others say, you will miss the mark. Focus
on essentials. Think things through carefully. Take nothing for granted. If
you want to find the truth you must look beneath the surface. Do not make
snap judgments. Be guided by what you most deeply feel to be right. Do not
look to the outside world to solve your problems for you. The answers lie
within. If you are to find them you must avoid being influenced by what is
superficial or trivial. Be true to yourself under all circumstances. Cooperate
with others and be supportive in your relationships. Your goodwill will be
returned.

An opportunity for personal growth

Self-development is highlighted here. The ancient symbol for this hexagram is that of a well. The issue, therefore, is one of drawing on the waters of life deep within you. People everywhere share the same emotional and spiritual needs for love, support, and inspiration. These are basic human values. To have clear water in your well is to demonstrate these values in your dealings with others. Acting in a truly humane fashion means accepting others without prejudice and relating to them as fellow travellers on the path of life. Ask yourself how you can best be of service in this situation. Let your motives be purely unselfish. Honour your own humanity and that of those you are involved with. Everybody will benefit.

Further aspects of the situation

SIX AT THE BEGINNING
You are completely neglecting your self-development. Life is all you have yet you are throwing it away. If you have no self-respect you cannot expect others to respect you. It is time you decided to start making something of yourself.

NINE IN THE SECOND PLACE
Because you are not serious enough about your life, you are frittering away your time in trivialities. If you do not develop your abilities they will grow rusty, like old machinery. You will then be of little use to anybody. Start realizing your worth.

NINE IN THE THIRD PLACE
Although you have a great deal to offer, your abilities are not being put to good use. This is a great loss to all concerned. If your value were to be recognized, everybody would benefit.

SIX IN THE FOURTH PLACE
You must put your life in order. Take time to consider your priorities, perhaps acquire new skills and generally work on your self-development.

153

It means that at present you cannot play an active part in the situation. Nor can you achieve your goals. But taking time out now will equip you to deal with life all the more effectively in the longer term.

NINE IN THE FIFTH PLACE
You have the potential to be a source of strength and wisdom which others can draw on. The important thing is to make sure that your abilities are used.

SIX AT THE TOP
Because you are generous and open-minded, you are an unfailing source of strength to those who have dealings with you. Your humane outlook will bring you very good fortune.

49

Total Transformation

'And no man putteth new wine into old bottles; else the new wine will burst the bottles, and be spilled, and the bottles shall perish. But new wine must be put into new bottles; and both are preserved.'

Luke, 5

Drastic change is indicated. There is no longer room in your life for anything which is outdated and/or does not serve your best interests. It is a case of off with the old and on with the new. Do not hesitate to make essential changes to your life-style and environment. They need to reflect who you are now rather than who you used to be. But you must proceed with care. Radical change will be destructive unless it is carried out in the appropriate way and at the right time. Think things through carefully. Because many aspects of your life will be transformed, there are far-reaching implications not only for yourself but for others who are involved. You must enlist their support. Discuss the issues in detail and address any doubts or fears they may have. If you go about the changes in the correct way, the outcome will be highly successful.

An opportunity for personal growth

Do not be surprised if you are experiencing a complete change of mind and heart. You may well be questioning long-standing ideas which you have previously taken for granted. Beliefs you have cherished in the past may no longer be relevant to your life as it is now. As you question what it is you really value, your attitudes and your expectations could change quite drastically. It is as though you were sloughing off an old skin in order to reveal more of who you really are. It is an exciting process but also one which can make you fearful of losing your security. Do not worry. By having the courage to live your life more fully, you can only gain in terms of feeling secure within yourself.

Further aspects of the situation

NINE AT THE BEGINNING
You are not sure whether it is the right time to act. Wait until it is obvious that you have no alternative.

SIX IN THE SECOND PLACE
Change is necessary and now is the time to go ahead. Make your plans, think things through and keep firmly in mind what you want the outcome to be. As conditions could change quite radically, you must feel prepared within yourself for a new situation. Taking action now will bring good fortune.

NINE IN THE THIRD PLACE
Make no hasty moves. The time to act has not yet come. Wait until it's quite obvious that change is essential. Even then, go ahead only if you have taken into consideration what this will mean for all concerned. You must have the full support of everybody involved.

NINE IN THE FOURTH PLACE
Radical change will usher in a new era. All will go well provided that your motives for taking action are correct. Change must not be made simply for its own sake or for purely selfish reasons. Others will only accept

the new conditions if they can see that what you are doing is fair and reasonable. Make sure that you yourself are adequately prepared for the new situation.

NINE IN THE FIFTH PLACE
Conditions are perfect for you to bring about a fundamental transformation. You know intuitively just what you must do. This is so clear to you that you do not even need to consult the *I Ching*. Because others recognize that you are right, they trust you and support your actions.

SIX AT THE TOP
You have gone as far as you can in making radical change. Be content with what you have achieved. Do not try to push matters further. Instead, work on details so as to consolidate your position. Take only such steps as are necessary to make sure that the new conditions will last.

50

The Cauldron

```
—— — ——
——————————
——————————
——————————
—— — ——
```

'There's only one real sin, and that is to persuade oneself that the second-best is anything but the second-best.'
Doris Lessing, *The Golden Notebook*

Make the most of your natural gifts. Polish up your skills. By putting them at the service of others, you can make an outstanding contribution to the situation. Fulfil your responsibilities to the best of your ability. Do not be materialistic in your aims and outlook. Great success is indicated but not as a result of pursuing wealth and status. Put aside self-interest in favour of more spiritual values such as kindness and generosity. Let these form the basis of your actions. Be sensitive to the needs of those around you. Do what you can to be useful. You can be a source of inspiration and strength to others. Because you have so much to offer, people will recognize your worth. Everybody will benefit.

An opportunity for personal growth

The ancient image for this hexagram is a cauldron, or sacred vessel which held the food for special offerings. What does this mean for you? Your current situation contains all the raw ingredients or potential out of which something very valuable can emerge. It is up to you to 'cook' these up into something worthwhile. The first step is to accept the present conditions whole-heartedly. Do not waste time running after something else. Focus on what is happening in the here and now. Take advantage of any opportunity you are presented with to develop and demonstrate your abilities. Be open to possibilities. Whatever you try to avoid or ignore will remain 'uncooked' and of little benefit to anybody. But your efforts to make something special of the situation will bring great rewards.

Further aspects of the situation

SIX AT THE BEGINNING

Although you lack experience or feel inadequate, you can in fact accomplish a great deal. But you must be open-minded and prepared to learn. This means putting aside your preconceived ideas about what is and is not possible.

NINE IN THE SECOND PLACE

Certain people may resent the good fortune you are enjoying. Do not allow this to concern you. Their envy cannot harm you. Nobody can take away what is rightfully yours.

NINE IN THE THIRD PLACE

At present, others do not recognize the value of what you have to offer. Your abilities therefore remain unused. This is a waste of valuable resources. But do not lose heart. Believe in yourself. In due course, the situation will change and all will go well for you.

NINE IN THE FOURTH PLACE
You are being unrealistic about what it is possible for you to achieve. Because you lack judgment and a sense of perspective, you dream of impossibly high goals. In the meantime, you are not using to best effect the abilities you do have.

SIX IN THE FIFTH PLACE
A well-balanced attitude will enable you to make the most of the situation. If you do the right thing in the right way, everything will fall into place. Remain modest and approachable and you will attract people who can help you to make progress.

NINE AT THE TOP
Your heart is in the right place. Because you act from the highest motives, you have an enormous amount to offer. Your contribution will benefit everybody concerned. All your efforts will meet with success.

51

Shock

___ ___
___ ___
_____

___ ___
___ ___
_____

'When an inner situation is not made conscious, it appears
outside as fate.'

C. G. Jung

An unexpected turn of events has shaken you to the core. Being unprepared,
you react with fear, possibly panic. But once you have recovered from the
initial shock, you will see that everything has happened for the best. Try
to stay calm. The outcome of this situation is a positive one. It may be
that you have been going about something in quite the wrong way. If so,
the upheaval will give you a chance to change direction. Possibly you have
been carrying too large a burden in some area of your life. One result of
the shake-up will be to remove it. This will free you to relax and take a
more optimistic view of things. As new possibilities beckon, your situation
will open up in a much more enjoyable way. You will emerge a stronger,
wiser and happier person.

An opportunity for personal growth

There are forces at work in your psyche which you cannot control. They belong to a deeper and wiser part of yourself. Sometimes it is essential to change an aspect of your life. This is often the case if you are in a situation which is wrong for you or is stagnating. If you resist change, your unconscious wisdom may give you a push by causing a disturbance in your life. The shock you have experienced may therefore be a way of forcing necessary change on you. Ask yourself what you can learn from it. Do you need to change your attitude towards someone or something? If you are prepared to rise to the challenge, then the shock will indeed have served a positive purpose. And life, after all, will never be totally predictable. If you can keep calm in the face of upheaval and respond in a creative way, it will do wonders for your self-confidence.

Further aspects of the situation

NINE AT THE BEGINNING
You have been deeply shaken by what has happened and may feel apprehensive about the future. But what looks on the surface like bad luck is actually a blessing in disguise. In the end you will be in a much better position.

SIX IN THE SECOND PLACE
You cannot stop the current upheaval. Trying to fight it would therefore be pointless. Accept your losses without attempting to recover them at this stage. In due course you will retrieve them.

SIX IN THE THIRD PLACE
Do not panic in the face of sudden upheaval. If you can stay calm and collected, you will see the positive options which are open to you.

NINE IN THE FOURTH PLACE
Shock has knocked you off balance so that you feel incapable of action. If you are to make progress, you must gather your wits and think clearly.

You need to find out what it is you must learn from this turn of events. Otherwise the situation will stagnate.

SIX IN THE FIFTH PLACE
Life seems to be dealing you one blow after another. Refuse to think of yourself as a helpless victim of circumstances. Stay cool, calm and well-organized. Keep your goal firmly in mind. Do what you can with the resources available to you. In the end you will in fact lose nothing.

SIX AT THE TOP
The disastrous events have caused widespread agitation. You must stand back from the situation and stay calm. Do not allow yourself to be affected by other people's fear. Go your own way. This may make you the object of gossip and criticism. But you must do what is in your own best interests.

52

Living in the Present

```
___   ___
___   ___
_____
___   ___
```

'You're only here for a short visit. Don't hurry. Don't worry. And be sure to smell the flowers along the way.'

Walter C. Hagen

The most pressing issue for you right now is to find peace of mind. You have arrived at the limits of what you can do. Now you must stop and reflect. Nothing can be gained by worrying about your problems, aims, achievements or whatever else is currently preoccupying you. Anxiety is not a good basis from which to make decisions. Whereas a calm, centred approach enables you to connect with deeper levels of yourself. In that state of mind you will intuitively make the right choices. You will have a sense of the most appropriate action to take in any situation. So focus on being present in the here and now. Do not dwell in the past. Yesterday has gone and cannot be retrieved. Tomorrow has yet to come and worrying will not change it. All that matters is to be firmly anchored in today, responding to each situation as it arises.

An opportunity for personal growth

The ancient symbol belonging to this hexagram is that of the mountain, the very essence of stillness. The message is that to be truly still is to be solidly grounded in the present moment. We all have deep within us an inner 'knower' to which we can look for guidance. But everyday life is full of distractions which prevent us from being in touch with this natural wisdom. To gain access to it needs a relaxed and quiet mind. This has always been recognized as a most difficult state to achieve. Meditation and yoga are time-honoured methods, as are the martial arts. They help take your focus off the outside world so that you become centred inside yourself. But anything which helps you to experience inner stillness will, with regular practice, be beneficial. The calmer you become, the stronger and more self-reliant you will feel.

Further aspects of the situation

SIX AT THE BEGINNING
The situation is only just beginning to unfold. If you are at all doubtful about taking action at this time, do not do so. Before making any move, you need to be quite certain which direction you are going in. Provided that your motives are unselfish, all will be well.

SIX IN THE SECOND PLACE
You are moving in the wrong direction. Instead of making your own choices, you are complying with somebody else's wishes. This unhappy state of affairs will not bring you success. You cannot stop somebody else moving down an obviously wrong path but you can choose not to follow them along it. Be true to yourself.

NINE IN THE THIRD PLACE
Don't try and force anything to a conclusion before the time is ripe. You may be feeling frustrated by the apparent lack of progress. Acknowledge these feelings but do not allow your behaviour to be controlled by them. Action taken because you are restless will lead to trouble. It is in your best interests to calm down and relax.

165

SIX IN THE FOURTH PLACE
Do not be impulsive. It is essential to stay cool, calm and collected. Doubts and fears may arise. Do not act on them. Wait until your mind is peaceful before you make decisions. Meditation is a good antidote to negative thoughts, as is any activity which helps you to switch off.

SIX IN THE FIFTH PLACE
Choose your words carefully. Once spoken, you cannot take them back. Avoid thoughtless remarks. If you want what you say to be effective, be sure to engage your brain before opening your mouth. You will then have no reason to regret what you say.

NINE AT THE TOP
If you have emotional stability and peace of mind, nothing can throw you off balance. Your self-possession will attract good fortune and be of benefit to whatever you are involved in. Stay deeply centred within yourself.

53

Gradual Development

```
━━━━━━━━━━━
━━━━  ━━━━
━━━━━━━━━━━
━━━━  ━━━━
━━━━━━━━━━━
━━━━  ━━━━
```

'Married in haste, we may repent at leisure.'
William Congreve

Patience is the keynote of this hexagram. You are counselled against taking hasty or premature action. The situation is compared to the traditional period of engagement before a marriage. In other words, events must be allowed to develop gradually. This will enable you to lay the firm foundations necessary for long-term and ongoing success. If you are greedy for immediate results, you may perhaps achieve something in the short term – but it is unlikely to last. Do not attempt to manipulate the situation to suit your own ends. Trust that matters will unfold in exactly the right way and to your ultimate benefit. At the same time, allowing things to develop gradually does not mean that you are without influence. If you are friendly, considerate and adaptable, you will have a positive effect on all concerned. This will help to create the best possible conditions for further progress.

An opportunity for personal growth

The slow progress of the situation may be frustrating. Resist the temptation to force matters to a head. Stay calm and centred. Do not lose sight of your goal or allow circumstances to disturb your equilibrium. Without being militant, stand up for what you feel to be right. A gentle but firm approach will win respect and meet with a favourable response. One of the symbols belonging to the original text of this hexagram is the wild goose. These birds emigrate according to the seasons and were thought to mate for life. They therefore came to represent faithfulness and stability. These are the qualities which the situation requires you to develop. Traditional ways of doing things are the most appropriate at this time.

Further aspects of the situation

SIX AT THE BEGINNING
Because the best course of action is not yet clear, you lack confidence in your ability to deal with the situation. Any attempts you do make at progress meet with criticism from others. However, these difficulties serve a useful purpose in that they prevent you from pushing ahead too hastily. By exercising caution now, you ensure success in the longer term.

SIX IN THE SECOND PLACE
You are now in a more secure position and can feel relaxed and optimistic. Sharing your good fortune with others adds to your own enjoyment.

NINE IN THE THIRD PLACE
Be patient. Otherwise you are liable to do something you will regret. To avoid causing trouble for yourself or others, you must exercise self-control. It would be very unwise to be drawn into a conflict. Allow the situation to develop naturally. If you must become involved, do only what is absolutely necessary to protect your own position.

168

SIX IN THE FOURTH PLACE

The situation, although relatively stable, does not feel right for you. Fortunately, this is a temporary state of affairs. There will be a change for the better. In the meantime, stay calm and accept the current position philosophically.

NINE IN THE FIFTH PLACE

Certain people may envy the extent of your progress. The resulting misunderstandings create barriers between yourself and others, making you feel isolated. Be patient. In due course all the difficulties will be resolved to your satisfaction.

NINE AT THE TOP

As a result of gradual, unremitting progress, you have achieved something of great value. Now you are in a position to help others who feel inspired by your example.

54

Playing a Subordinate Role

'I am certain of nothing but the holiness of the heart's affections and the truth of the imagination.'

Keats

In spite of the contribution you are making to the situation, your value as an individual is not being recognized. There is nothing you can do to influence matters. If you try to be assertive, you will meet with no response. Do your best to adapt to circumstances without expecting too much. Go quietly about your business and keep yourself to yourself. Although you are in a subservient position you can nevertheless act with dignity. Accept the reality of the situation and do what is required without resentment. If you are faced with a choice to be made, take care. Beware of being manipulated by others. If you are enquiring about a relationship issue, it is very important that you do not try to control the situation. Bear in mind that wanting to possess somebody exclusively is not the same as loving them. This attitude cannot ultimately bring happiness.

An opportunity for personal growth

Taking a long-term view of matters will enable you to keep a sense of perspective. Do not allow disagreements to undermine a relationship. They are simply part of an ongoing process and will pass if you do not make a big issue of them. Do not let pride or jealousy trip you up. Take responsibility for the atmosphere you create. You will get far better results by being warm and affectionate than by insisting on what you believe to be your rights. Do not criticize or complain. Be tactful and kind. By becoming less dependent on others, you will acquire inner freedom and a greater sense of your own worth.

Further aspects of the situation

NINE AT THE BEGINNING
Because of conditions beyond your control, you have only very limited influence. Make the most of it by being helpful and tactful. Avoid any hint of aggression.

NINE IN THE SECOND PLACE
Matters have not turned out as anticipated. Do not allow disappointment to make you bitter or resentful. Have faith in yourself and remain committed to what you believe to be true.

SIX IN THE THIRD PLACE
To get what you want will mean compromising yourself. This would have a disastrous effect on your self-esteem. Be patient and wait for a better opportunity.

NINE IN THE FOURTH PLACE
You are right to turn down opportunities which do not feel appropriate for you. To others, it may seem that you are being left behind, but you must be true to yourself. In due course you will reap the rewards of your current unwillingness to compromise.

SIX IN THE FIFTH PLACE

No matter how much ability you have, or how strong your position may be, keep out of the spotlight. Do not demand attention or try to control the situation. Focus on how you can best be of service. Resist any temptation to compete with others in order to prove how wonderful you are.

SX AT THE TOP

Without a heartfelt commitment to what you are doing, you will not succeed. If you merely go through the motions you are wasting your time and energy. In relationships, do your best not to be jealous or possessive.

55

Abundance

```
___   ___
___   ___
_____
___   ___
_____
```

'My cup runneth over.'
Psalm 23

The conditions are such that you can fulfil your potential and realize your goals. Relationships and projects will thrive. Success is assured. Be open and generous. Life will continue to give to you in the measure which you give to others. Only if you hold back, will the flow of abundance to you begin to dry up. Give for the sake of giving and not in order to get something back. A truly warm and generous heart will bring its own rewards. Sharing with others will have a stimulating effect on your own life, whereas meanness of spirit will drain your energies. Take advantage of favourable circumstances to resolve outstanding problems. Look carefully and objectively at the facts before taking the appropriate action. If there are problems to settle in a relationship, be kind but firm.

An opportunity for personal growth

Count your blessings. Do not allow your enjoyment of the situation to be clouded by anxiety about the future. It is true that nothing stays the same for ever. But the best insurance against future problems is to build on your current position of strength. Others are strongly influenced by your attitudes. You owe it to all concerned to be positive and optimistic. Do not worry about future loss or gain. Live fully in the here and now. Worrying about what has not yet happened will only serve to weaken you. Do what you feel to be right. Trust in your ability to cope with whatever the future may bring. Do not allow lurking doubts and fears to undermine your confidence.

Further aspects of the situation

NINE AT THE BEGINNING
You meet somebody of like mind, possibly by chance. It would be to your mutual advantage to work together for a specific purpose.

SIX IN THE SECOND PLACE
Despite your obvious abilities you cannot make progress. Circumstances are such that others dislike or mistrust you. Do not try to force the issue. Be patient and sincere. Have faith in yourself. In the end, your influence will make itself felt. Those who matter will realize your worth.

NINE IN THE THIRD PLACE
However capable you are, it is impossible for you to achieve what you would like to. Through no fault of your own, you are prevented from taking effective action. Be patient. The situation will change in due course.

NINE IN THE FOURTH PLACE
Progress has been blocked. Now you have an opportunity to connect with those who can help you to get things moving. Enthusiastic action combined with sound judgment will produce a successful outcome.

SIX IN THE FIFTH PLACE

Excellent advice is available. Be modest and willing to accept the help you need. The end result will be extremely successful and beneficial to all concerned.

SIX AT THE TOP

You are warned against becoming so self-obsessed that you are unwilling to share your blessings with others. Beware of growing arrogant and forgetting those who have supported you. If you insist on keeping everything for yourself, you will become totally isolated.

56

Stranger in a Strange Land

```
━━━  ━ ━
━━━━━━━
━━━━━━━
━━━  ━ ━
━━━  ━ ━
```

'If a man be gracious and courteous to strangers, it shews he is a citizen of the world.'

Francis Bacon

The current situation is temporary. Do not let yourself get too deeply involved. Be prepared for change. Avoid making a commitment to any particular person or situation. Consider this as a time when you can gather information, expand your horizons and make discoveries about yourself and others. Keep your wits about you. Be practical and willing to adapt to whatever changes may occur. When meeting new people, be respectful but also cautious at first and a little reserved. Associate only with those whose motives you feel you can trust. Do not compromise your self-respect in an effort to win acceptance. If you are sincere and courteous, the right people will assist you. Be sure to express your gratitude to anyone who gives you a helping hand. Where possible, be helpful in return.

An opportunity for personal growth

You are wandering in unfamiliar territory without a map. Your journey is about exploring new ideas and possibilities, perhaps even a new identity. You will be quite safe as long as you observe certain ground rules. Whatever the situation, treat it as a learning experience. Most importantly, be self-reliant. Because circumstances could change at any time, you cannot depend too much on others. This means that your only true security lies within. You are therefore thrown back on your own resources. This gives you an opportunity to develop your ability to cope with the unfamiliar. If you can be at ease with yourself regardless of circumstances, you will respond to whatever happens in the most appropriate way.

Further aspects of the situation

SIX AT THE BEGINNING
Do not try to win approval by demeaning yourself. You will succeed only in inviting contempt and ridicule. Keep your dignity and people will respect you. Avoid frittering away your energy or resources on trivial matters.

SIX IN THE SECOND PLACE
If you are modest and reserved, people will want to help you. They will be attracted by your quiet confidence and self-possession.

NINE IN THE THIRD PLACE
Beware of interfering in what is not your business. Guard against being quick-tempered or arrogant. If others find your behaviour offensive, you could lose their support and destroy what you have achieved so far.

NINE IN THE FOURTH PLACE
Although you have accomplished a certain amount, you have not arrived at your goal. You would like to hold on to what you have achieved so far and make your position secure. Yet if you are to make further progress, the situation will have to change. The answer is to move slowly and cautiously.

SIX IN THE FIFTH PLACE
Your task is completed. No further difficulties stand in your way. Although your journey has involved some hardship you have used your abilities to best advantage. People have finally recognized your worth. Now you can successfully establish yourself in the new situation.

NINE AT THE TOP
If you are careless you risk losing something essential to your security. Value what you have by taking care of it properly. Do not be selfish. Show consideration for others and be willing to adapt.

57

Gentle Influence

```
━━━━  ━━━━
━━━━  ━━━━
━━━━    ━━━━
━━━━  ━━━━
━━━━  ━━━━
━━━━    ━━━━
```

'For the gentle wind does move Silently, invisibly.'
William Blake

You can influence the situation only in subtle ways at present. You must therefore be quite clear in your own mind exactly what it is you want. Keep this aim constantly in mind. For the time being, be content to remain in the background. From there you can exert a gentle but steady influence on the situation. Because this is a slow process you must be confident in your ability to achieve your aim. Be alert to any opportunity which will help to further your cause. Just as a tree sways in the wind, you must find a way of adapting to circumstances rather than struggling against them. Do not be aggressive or try to take control. Patience, flexibility and an open mind will help you to make the most intelligent use of circumstances.

An opportunity for personal growth

Your challenge here is to be clear about your intent. The mind is immensely powerful. If you have a strong intention to accomplish something and constantly channel your resources in that direction, sooner or later you will succeed. Doors will open to help you on your way. Opportunities for progress will mysteriously present themselves. You must be determined to make a long-term commitment and have the strength of mind to follow it through. And it is essential to believe in what you are doing. If you have doubts about whether your goal is worthwhile, your uncertainty will act as a self-fulfilling prophecy.

Further aspects of the situation

SIX AT THE BEGINNING
You must use your will-power. Refuse to be ruled by the doubts and fears which make you hesitant. Be single-minded. Make a decision and stick to it. It is a matter of self-discipline.

NINE IN THE SECOND PLACE
There are secret influences at work which are acting against you. They must be identified. Once they have been brought out into the light of day and examined, they will lose their power. Question your own motives and those of others. Look for hidden agendas. Get help with this if necessary.

NINE IN THE THIRD PLACE
You are right to weigh up the pros and cons of the matter. But you cannot hope to know in advance all the results of acting in a particular way. In the end you must come to a decision. The more you worry about the outcome, the less confident you will feel about taking action.

SIX IN THE FOURTH PLACE
Put doubt and hesitation behind you. It is time to take vigorous action. You will be extremely successful in getting what you need.

NINE IN THE FIFTH PLACE

A change for the better is indicated. Think carefully about what you propose to do. Once you have embarked upon a new course of action, keep a close eye on developments. Allow time for a transition period. When you can see the situation improving, you can be sure that you are on the right track.

NINE AT THE TOP

You have delved far enough into all the whys and wherefores of the situation. If you go any further with this, you will have no energy left to actually do anything about it. Make the best decision you can and proceed to act on it.

58

Joy in Communicating

```
——  ——
————————
——  ——
————————
```

'He who bends to himself a Joy doth the winged life destroy;
But he who kisses the Joy as it flies Lives in Eternity's sunrise.'
William Blake

In this situation, the emphasis is on a free flow of communication in a spirit
of goodwill. Be optimistic and outgoing. Others can help you to accomplish
your aims. If you approach people in a friendly way, you will get a positive
response. Discussion must take place in an atmosphere which encourages
freedom of expression. If people are confident that their views will be given
a fair hearing, ideas will flow freely. Communication then becomes enjoyable
and stimulating for all. You can learn from others and they from you. New
approaches can be found and creative thinking generated. When people are
enjoying themselves, troubles begin to fade into the background. With the
support and encouragement of others, even the most difficult or disagreeable
tasks will seem less problematic. A most successful outcome is indicated.

An opportunity for personal growth

You cannot run after joy. The more you try to catch it, the more elusive it becomes. Pursuing it will at best bring moments of pleasure which do not last. Do not rely on other people or on particular circumstances for your happiness. Over-dependence on anything outside yourself is bound to create anxiety. As a result of feeling insecure, you may try very hard to control whoever or whatever is involved. But to approach life in this way is to invite disappointment. If you want to experience joy from within, you must create the right conditions for it. Be true to yourself. Trust that you have within you the resources you need. Take pleasure in living life as it comes. Focus on giving rather than getting. You have it in you to be a source of inspiration and encouragement to others.

Further aspects of the situation

NINE AT THE BEGINNING

Be content with life as it is. You do not need to look further than where you are in order to feel good about life. Do not make demands on others. Rest assured that you have everything you need to make you happy, just as you are.

NINE IN THE SECOND PLACE

Be sincere and true to yourself. Don't waste time and energy on activities which are inappropriate for you in order to be 'one of the crowd'. Success will be a result of putting a proper value on yourself.

SIX IN THE THIRD PLACE

True and lasting joy comes from within. If you plunge headlong into mindless distractions you will certainly fill up your time, but such empty pleasures will bring you no real fulfilment. Do not demean yourself in an attempt to further your ambitions.

NINE IN THE FOURTH PLACE

In which direction does your happiness lie? The fact that you are indecisive indicates that you don't yet know what your real values are. If you are looking for peace of mind, follow the path which will give you lasting benefit. The alternative is to allow yourself to be seduced by temporary pleasures. But these will not ultimately bring you joy.

NINE IN THE FIFTH PLACE

It would be easy for you to place your trust in unscrupulous people. Or you may perhaps be considering becoming involved in a dubious situation. Be very careful. Keep your wits about you. Use all your powers of discrimination to make sure that you are not in danger of being exploited.

SIX AT THE TOP

If you depend on the outside world to provide you with happiness, you will be blown about like a feather in the wind. Try not to seek approval from others. Do not allow yourself to be swept along by circumstances. Maintain your integrity. If you lose touch with yourself, you will not attract the right people.

59

Obstacles Fade Away

```
━━━━  ━━━━
━━━━  ━━━━
━━━━  ━━━━
━━━━  ━━━━
━━━━  ━━━━
━━━━  ━━━━
```

'To err is human; to forgive, divine.'
Alexander Pope

Blockages to progress can now be removed. Areas of misunderstanding or uncertainty can be clarified. You must tackle any issues which keep you from communicating freely and sincerely with others. Nothing will be achieved until harmony is restored between people. Where there is antagonism in your environment, you must set about the process of reconciliation. Factions must be broken up. Be gentle and tactful. An over-assertive manner will serve only to harden other people's defences. You are more likely to succeed if you bear in mind the wider picture. The truth is that your own well-being cannot be separated from that of other people. If one person suffers, all concerned are affected in some way. At the very deepest level, all are part of one human family. Do not be deceived into believing there is no such thing as society so that only the individual counts. To hold this view is short-sighted and indicates a lack of spiritual awareness.

An opportunity for personal growth

Before you can tackle obstructions in your outer environment you must first look at the emotional blockages which isolate you from others. If you are holding on to anger or resentment, bring them out into the open. Light needs to be shed on areas of darkness or confusion. Do not bear grudges. They create obstacles to further progress, whereas forgiveness clears the air and opens the way forward. Try to be flexible and appreciate other people's point of view. Give up unrealistic expectations which nobody – least of all yourself – could possibly live up to. Have compassion, for yourself as well as others. Do not allow selfishness to prevail over love.

Further aspects of the situation

SIX AT THE BEGINNING
A conflict is beginning. Do not allow it to develop. Act promptly to reconcile the differences which have arisen. At this early stage the matter can be easily resolved.

NINE IN THE SECOND PLACE
A feeling of being alienated from others must not be allowed to develop any further. This unhealthy state of mind is damaging to your overall well-being. You must do something to help yourself recover your goodwill and sense of humour. Making an effort to help somebody else could do the trick.

SIX IN THE THIRD PLACE
Try to stop thinking in terms of your own self-interest. Aim to drop the defences which make you feel separate from others. Your fulfilment now lies in working for the benefit of all. It means putting aside all personal and selfish concerns. You will have no cause to regret this.

SIX IN THE FOURTH PLACE
You must rise above your own personal interests and prejudices. Great success will be the result of a commitment to working for the general well-being. Although this may take you out of your own immediate circle, you will receive a great deal of support.

NINE IN THE FIFTH PLACE
Matters are at a standstill. Take the initiative in helping to put things right. You have it in you to create a breakthrough. A completely new approach is needed. This will take every ounce of effort you can make plus all the resources at your disposal.

NINE AT THE TOP
Matters are at a crisis. You must protect both your own interests and those of people who depend on you. Do whatever you have to, even if this means leaving the situation altogether.

60

Self-Control

```
═══   ═══
══════════
═══   ═══
══════════
```

'It is in self-limitation that a master first shows himself.'
Goethe

Do not go to extremes or try to take on too much. In this situation,
you must decide for yourself what your limitations are. Keep the balance
between wanting too much and being willing to settle for too little. If
you are too fearful to make a move, nothing can be achieved. But if you
are over-ambitious, you could fall flat on your face. Decide where your
responsibilities lie. Make a commitment to them. Do not expect more of
yourself than you know is realistic. And don't demand more of others than
they are capable of giving. Be discriminating in your approach to people.
Do not be over-friendly, on the one hand, or too reserved on the other.
Keep control of your financial affairs. Do not be extravagant. At the same
time, avoid being tight-fisted.

An opportunity for personal growth

You may dream of doing many things. But life is too short to do everything you would like to. You must choose a direction from the possibilities open to you. What matters is to have an aim which can be turned into reality. Otherwise your dreams will remain mere fantasies. Be realistic. Decide what you are capable of and how far you are willing to push yourself. On this basis, you can set yourself achievable goals. If you try to do the impossible you will only exhaust yourself and lose a great deal of confidence into the bargain. By limiting yourself to what is manageable you can acquire new skills and knowledge. An added bonus will be the pleasure of doing something really well.

Further aspects of the situation

NINE AT THE BEGINNING
You would like to accomplish something but too much stands in your way at present. The way to strengthen your position is by not trying to push ahead. Stay within the limits of what is possible.

NINE IN THE SECOND PLACE
Be prepared to take action as soon as the right moment comes. Do not allow doubt or anxiety to prevent you from seizing the opportunity. Remember that he or she who hesitates is lost.

SIX IN THE THIRD PLACE
If you don't exercise self-control, you will have no one but yourself to blame for the consequences.

SIX IN THE FOURTH PLACE
Be content to adapt to the current conditions. Do not waste energy by trying to do more than the situation will allow. A flexible attitude will bring you success.

NINE IN THE FIFTH PLACE
Do the best you can with the resources available to you. Set an example by accepting current restrictions with good grace. Do not expect others to do anything which you are not prepared to do yourself.

SIX AT THE TOP
Do not be too hard on yourself or on others. If you have to be extremely disciplined for a short time in order to make an important change, then do so. But do not let this state of affairs continue beyond what is absolutely necessary. Too much restriction leads to rebellion.

61

The Power of Inner Truth

≡ ≡

'This above all – to thine own self be true,
And it must follow, as the night the day,
Thou canst not then be false to any man.'
Shakespeare, *Hamlet*

The way to influence this situation is through your commitment to the truth. Even the most difficult people will respond to somebody they sense is genuinely sincere. But to be successful you must find the right approach. It is a matter of establishing rapport. First you must put aside any preconceived ideas. Be completely open and receptive to whoever is involved. Assume you know nothing about them and that you therefore have everything to learn. In this way, you will be able to step across the barriers between you and look at life from the other person's point of view. Once you understand what matters to them, you will know how to establish contact. By speaking from your heart, you will make your influence felt. If you go about things in this way, you will succeed in handling even the most difficult situations.

An opportunity for personal growth

The only way to create lasting change is by being true to yourself. Unless you live with integrity to yourself, your life will be shallow and have little meaning. You must learn to be fiercely courageous. Be prepared to stand up for the truth through thick and thin. Do not flatter others or try to impress or manipulate them. Instead, learn to accept people as they are. Put aside all judgment and criticism. Watch, listen and above all, keep an open mind. Try to appreciate all the circumstances involved. At the same time, you must make it clear that you are not a pushover. Do not hesitate to speak the truth, even if it means taking a solitary stand. The fact that you may not have interests in common must not deter you. Deep and permanent bonds between people are based not on mutual self-interest but on truth.

Further aspects of the situation

NINE AT THE BEGINNING
Be sincere. Let your actions be based on what you truly feel to be right. Do not rely on anything outside yourself. The result would be confusion. Do not become involved in anything of a dubious nature.

NINE IN THE SECOND PLACE
Be absolutely genuine in all you say and do. If what you express is the truth, your words will influence the hearts and minds of all those who are in tune with you. Relationships developed on this basis will be deep and lasting. Great happiness will result.

SIX IN THE THIRD PLACE
If you depend on other people to make you feel strong and self-confident, you will be deeply affected by their moods and opinions. You could feel very happy one day and extremely miserable the next. It would benefit you to learn to know your own mind and be more self-reliant.

SIX IN THE FOURTH PLACE
Your loyalty must be to what you genuinely feel to be the truth. Put selfish concerns aside and resist any pressure to take sides. You would benefit from the guidance of someone wiser and more experienced than yourself.

NINE IN THE FIFTH PLACE
If you are so deeply committed to the truth that it permeates all you say and do, you can help to transform the situation. Everybody concerned will be influenced by your sincerity. There will be an extremely fortunate outcome.

NINE AT THE TOP
Watch what you say. Do not boast or make promises you cannot live up to. If you are over-ambitious you will cause serious problems for yourself.

62

Attention to Detail

　—— ——
　—————
　—————
　—— ——

'It has long been an axiom of mine that the little things are infinitely
the most important.'

Sir Arthur Conan Doyle

Nothing of great significance can be accomplished at this time. Do not even
attempt to undertake important matters. You do not have enough power to
achieve as much as you would like to. You will benefit from keeping a low
profile and attending to the business at hand. Go calmly about your daily
routine. Occupy yourself with ordinary, everyday matters. Do not consider
any task as being beneath you. You cannot be too thorough in your attention
to detail. Know your limitations. Do not over-extend yourself or try to take
on more than you are truly capable of. If you try to fly too high, you will
lose control. Keep your feet on the ground and enjoy the simple things of
life. Take no risks. Do not be too proud or ambitious. This will set people
against you. Whereas if you are modest, they will be willing to help you.

An opportunity for personal growth

Your challenge is to accept the current situation with good grace and in a spirit of humility. Keep both pride and ambition firmly under control. This in no way implies losing your dignity. On the contrary, the situation demands all your powers of self-restraint. Be particularly careful to show courtesy and consideration to others. Do not make unreasonable demands or allow frustration to cause you to over-react. This is not the appropriate time to push yourself into the limelight. Do not put on an act or try to impress others. If you are unpretentious, your relationships will flourish. The situation is a test of your patience and stability.

Further aspects of the situation

SIX AT THE BEGINNING
Stick to the tried and tested ways you know. You are not sufficiently prepared to take a major step forward. Wait until your have a wider understanding of the situation.

SIX IN THE SECOND PLACE
You are limited in what you can do. Stay with what is well within your capabilities. If you do the best you can with the resources available, all will be well.

NINE IN THE THIRD PLACE
Take care not to be over-confident. Unexpected difficulties could catch you unawares. Pay great attention to detail. Be very cautious and exercise good judgment.

NINE IN THE FOURTH PLACE
Do not make any attempt to reach your goal. Be extremely cautious. Trying to force the issue will put you in a risky position. Don't try to do more than you're capable of. This situation will not last for ever. In the meantime, be patient and keep strictly within the limits of what is possible.

SIX IN THE FIFTH PLACE

Although you have achieved a certain amount, you are not strong enough to do any more on your own. If you want to make further progress, you need help from people who have the relevant experience. Be respectful. Do not assume that whoever you approach will feel obliged to give you support.

SIX AT THE TOP

Do not try to fly too high. Know and respect your limitations. Don't try to impress. If you attempt to go beyond what is realistically possible, you will be asking for trouble.

63

Mission Accomplished

'I have fought a good fight, I have finished my course, I have kept the faith.'

2 Timothy

Everything seems to be in perfect order. You have basically done what you set out to do. Only the details remain to be finalized. It would be only too easy to sit back and relax, assuming that the situation will now take care of itself. But it will not. It is precisely at this stage that things can go wrong. In any aspect of life, keeping something at the peak of perfection takes work. If you let things slide, they simply go downhill. Pay great attention to detail. Be aware of where problems may arise unless you are careful. Take the appropriate precautions to prevent this happening. Forewarned is forearmed. If you are blessed with secure relationships, do not take them for granted. They too need care and attention if they are to remain stable.

An opportunity for personal growth

It is a rule of life that everything changes. Therefore nothing can remain as it is indefinitely. The fact that you have accomplished something does not mean that progress stops there. To consolidate your gains is like keeping the pot on the boil. You have to keep an eye on it. If the fire gets too low or the pot boils dry, you have problems. This means that you must keep your wits about you. Notice whatever needs to be done to keep your particular pot boiling merrily. If you become careless or lose motivation, the situation will begin to decline.

Further aspects of the situation

NINE AT THE BEGINNING
Progress is being made. But do not be tempted to push ahead too quickly in an effort to see results. Before you take any step, carefully consider what it may involve. If you act on impulse you run the risk of creating problems.

SIX IN THE SECOND PLACE
A problem causes a temporary delay but it is not serious. Do not try to press forward. Wait patiently. When you are meant to achieve something, nothing can ultimately prevent you.

NINE IN THE THIRD PLACE
You have achieved something very difficult. Be careful not to throw away the results of your hard work by involving someone who is unreliable or insufficiently skilled.

SIX IN THE FOURTH PLACE
Be on your guard. There may be hidden problems lurking. You cannot afford to take things easy or to be too soft with others.

NINE IN THE FIFTH PLACE
Be sincere. Avoid extravagance. Do not feel that you must go to great lengths to impress others. It is far better to do things simply but with real feeling. If your heart is in the right place, you will attract good fortune.

198

SIX AT THE TOP
Do not be content to simply stand back and admire what you have achieved so far. You cannot afford to rest on your laurels. If you let things slide, you could lose all you have gained. Keep on moving ahead.

64

Nearly Home and Dry

'For the times they are a-changin'!'
Bob Dylan

It is a difficult time. There is great potential for change to a much better situation, but nothing is settled yet. You must be determined to achieve your goal. The problem is knowing how to go about it in the best way. You are being pulled in different directions and must make sense of the confusion. Decisions have to be made. Yet nothing in your past experience can guide you in this instance. First, you must be absolutely clear in your own mind what you want the outcome to be. Make sure that each step you take leads you in that direction. Proceed with the utmost caution. Use your common sense. Be streetwise and adaptable. Stay on the alert for signs that your approach is not working. If this happens, stop and consider what might be a more effective way. Be very wary. Provided you take nothing for granted, success is guaranteed.

An opportunity for personal growth

Your ability to withstand pressure will be put to the test here. Because things could so easily go wrong, your position is precarious. Each move you make will have a significant effect on your prospects of success. Be very patient. Stay calm and centred. It will take time to resolve matters. Do not be tempted to take risks in an effort to hurry things along. It is at crucial times like this that all your fears and insecurities can surface. To counteract these, do not have unrealistic expectations of yourself. Just do the best you are capable of, one step at a time.

Further aspects of the situation

SIX AT THE BEGINNING
Don't be carried away by your enthusiasm to get results. By acting hastily, you could ruin everything. As yet, you are not in a position to understand what to do for the best. Hold back and do nothing.

NINE IN THE SECOND PLACE
Prepare yourself resolutely for taking the next step but do nothing as yet. The opportunity for action will come. Do not be impatient.

SIX IN THE THIRD PLACE
You are not in a strong enough position to handle the situation on your own. Do not even try to do so. The solution is to cut your losses, get some capable help and start again.

NINE IN THE FOURTH PLACE
You have a battle on your hands. There are difficult issues to be resolved before you can achieve your aim. The struggle may be with your own ego and the problems it creates for you, or with another person. Either way, it will take all your courage and will-power to win the fight. In the end your determination will be rewarded.

SIX IN THE FIFTH PLACE

You have won through. Your patience and determination have paid off. Now the way forward is clear. Others will recognize that what you have achieved is a splendid success. You will receive their confidence and support.

NINE AT THE TOP

Your aim is about to be accomplished. This is certainly something to celebrate. But do not get carried away. If over-excitement causes you to do something foolish, you will create problems for yourself. Others will no longer trust you.

Bibliography

If you are interested in reading more about the *I Ching* or consulting other versions, the following are recommended: *I Ching or Book of Changes*, translated from the Chinese by Richard Wilhelm and into English by Cary F. Baynes. This is a classic translation with a very interesting foreword by C. G. Jung.

The I Ching translated by Stephen Karcher and Rudolf Ritsema.
The I Ching Workbook by R. L. Wing.
The Book of Changes and the Unchanging Truth by Hua–Ching Ni.
A Guide to the I Ching by Carol K. Anthony.

The Names and Numbers of the Hexagrams

Chart for Identifying the Hexagrams

UPPER TRIGRAM / LOWER TRIGRAM	☰	☳	☵	☶	☷	☴	☲	☱
☰	1	34	5	26	11	9	14	43
☳	25	51	3	27	24	42	21	17
☵	6	40	29	4	7	59	64	47
☶	33	62	39	52	15	53	56	31
☷	12	16	8	23	2	20	35	45
☴	44	32	48	18	46	57	50	28
☲	13	55	63	22	36	37	30	49
☱	10	54	60	41	19	61	38	58